Henry Roelifsen Brinkerhoff

Nah-nee-ta

a tale of the Navajos

Henry Roelifsen Brinkerhoff

Nah-nee-ta
a tale of the Navajos

ISBN/EAN: 9783337023775

Printed in Europe, USA, Canada, Australia, Japan

Cover: Foto ©Thomas Meinert / pixelio.de

More available books at **www.hansebooks.com**

PREFACE.

The purpose of the author in giving this labor of real and fictitious things to the public may find expression better in a preface, probably, than elsewhere.

For a period of several years following close upon the war of the rebellion, he was stationed in Western New Mexico in the immediate vicinity of the country occupied by the Navajos, and became during that time largely acquainted with the customs and habits of this remarkable people.

Since that period a railroad has been built almost upon the Southern line of their reservation, and settlements of white people have been made upon all sides about them. Influenced by these means, many of their time-honored practices and customs have been largely modified or entirely abandoned.

A new people, virtually, has made its appearance in place of the old one, with entirely different views of life, and its duties. A people, it may be said, without practically a single national characteristic yet developed in this new transitional state.

The influences thus exerted have caused the young men to become skeptical of the teachings of their elders, and at the same time have made them slow to adopt the habits and practices of strangers.

The customs of the people before these changes occurred, will now only be preserved by means of unreliable legends.

Anticipating this result, the author endeavored during his residence near them, to obtain reliable information concerning their ancient customs and beliefs, in order that it might be preserved as a possible contribution to science.

The task proved to be a difficult one.

Such practices and evidences. of belief as fell under his personal observation, day after day, for long periods of time, alone seemed well substantiated. Information obtained through those who were able to converse with the Navajos in their own language, was in most cases meager, and often contradictory. The Indians seemed unable to understand why white men should want to know anything about their beliefs or practices. They usually became suspicious when questioned, and replied evasively or indefinitely.

In summing up all that had been gained after several years had elapsed, the author found that but few facts of interest to science had been acquired, which were sufficiently well corroborated to warrant the publication he had in view.

To the end, however, that his labors might not be entirely lost, he selected those best substantiated by the statements of the Navajos, and such as had fallen under his own personal observation, as the basis of a story of Navajo life. These may be summed up practically as follows:

In their savage state the Navajos believed in the existence of a Supreme Being, by whom the first Navajo was created. He was made from a living turkey, which alone of all animate things had survived a long period of rain and a consequent flood.

They believed that both men and women possessed souls, or spirits, but that the souls of brave warriors alone were immortal. The souls of the women went into live fish when they died. The souls of the warriors entered a land of trial after death, inhabited by a race of vicious big-eared pigmies, with whom they had frequent battles on their journey to the spirit-land. The souls that survived this journey eventually reached the shore of a great body of water and were taken to an island where a woman reigned, and where they lived eternally in the enjoyment of sensual pleasures.

The souls of warriors who were unable to stand the ordeal of personal encounters with the pigmies, perished forever.

They attributed bodily disease to the enmity of evil spirits.

They placed implicit faith, apparently, in the power of their medicine men to influence supernatural things, and to make curative preparations and charms.

They practiced cremation of the dead.

They lived usually in clans or large families, under the leadership of sub-chiefs, and wandered about with their flocks of sheep and herds of horses, over an immense region of country, a considerable portion of which they still hold as a reservation.

A head chief controlled all ordinary national affairs, and a war chief directed those pertaining to his special office.

They were by no means a taciturn people, except on formal occasions, or in the presence of strangers, neither were they unusually loquacious. They loved to talk, however, and their councils, at which public speaking was permitted, were always very popular.

A number of individuals among them possessed remarkable powers of eloquence. At a council held shortly after the war of the rebellion, between the Commissioners of the United States and the chiefs of the Nation, with the view of determining upon the articles of a treaty, the head chief, Barbon-ce-to, made an address of great power and eloquence. Influenced by this speech concessions were granted which the Commissioners had previously refused to admit. A few years later, the war chief, Manu-le-to, made an eloquent address before a council held upon some public business. A single paragraph from this address can be given. A distinguished officer of the army was present on this occasion as the representative of the Government, and Manu-le-to, referring to the campaign of General Carleton against the Navajos in 1863-4, said to the interpreter: "Say to the one-armed General that he well knows what then occurred. The war came upon the Navajos like a great strong wind, against which no man could stand. It blew the trees down and tore the grass up by the roots. It gathered the little stones in its way, and hurled them before it. The people breathed of the wind and they died."

They practiced polygamy, and young wives were obtained usually by purchase.

They were inveterate gamblers, and individuals often impoverished themselves at play. The women especially seemed delighted when engaged in some game of chance. After losing all they possessed, they not infrequently ventured their personal services as peons, for long periods of time.

They possessed large quantities of silver, and many of their trappings were richly ornamented with this precious metal.

They spent much of their time on horseback, and were confirmed wanderers. In time of peace, many individuals made their homes temporarily with the Utes and Apaches, or with the various Pueblos in Arizona and New Mexico.

They held their captives from the neighboring tribes, from Mexico and the settlements in the valley of the Rio Grande, in a state of peonage.

These embrace largely the results of the labors of the author, so far as they apply to the work now under consideration.

In conclusion, he expresses the hope that the story of Nah-nee-ta may not be found without interest to the reader, and that whatever influence it may exert, will be wholly for good.

NAH-NEE-TA.

NAH-NEE-TA.

I.

From one of the great cañons that take their origin near the Eastern limit of Arizona, and extend Westward through the intervening ranges of the Rocky Mountains into the great unexplored cañon of the Colorado, Barbon-ce-to, the head chief of the Navajos, had sent out his runners to the chiefs and the principal men of the several clans of the nation, inviting them to meet him in council.

The place designated by the head chief for the assembly had been used for such purpose, according to tribal traditions, from time immemorial. Here, during all the known history of the Navajos, their chiefs and principal men had assembled on all extraordinary occasions to take council with each other, and devise means for the general welfare of the nation.

The walls of the cañon rose to a sublime height, approaching each other near their summit, and shutting out forever the rays of the sun. At the base of the cañon, the walls had been worn away for a considerable distance by the action of the elements, until a vast amphitheatre had been formed.

This great vaulted space, ever full of strange echoes, hidden away down in the very bowels of the earth, inaccessible to man, except by a narrow passage at the opening of the cañon, was the sacred council chamber of the Navajos.

Barbon-ce-to had sent out his runners with all the formalities of time-honored custom. Each runner had been called separately before him, and instructed to proceed with all possible haste, to cease not in his journey, neither to sleep nor to eat until he had found the chief of a designated clan, and had placed in his hands the token of his mission. The head chief then took from his girdle or his necklace, some valuable and well-known personal ornament, a precious stone, or a large, rudely-carved button of silver, and presented it to the runner.

"Go now to my brother," he said, "and deliver into his hands this token, that he may know Barbon-ce-to has spoken, and may hasten himself to return it."

The runner, proud of his honorable mission, and the confidence reposed in him, hastened from the presence of the head chief, and was soon speeding away on his errand.

The most powerful clans of the nation dwelt to the North, along the clear waters of the San Juan, and the Cariso. Other clans dwelt to the Northwest, on the verdant banks of the Rio-de-Chelly, and others on the Northeast, in the well-watered valleys of the Chaco, and the Rio-de-la-Plata. One clan only, dwelt in the South. To each of these clans a runner had been sent.

From the Northward, the chiefs of the great clans would hasten to come down, in answer to the summons of the head chief, as had always been their custom. From the Southward, no one was expected, unless indeed it might be that the young chief Mariano would accept the invitation of Barbon-ce-to, and come up from the Rio Puerco to represent his clan in the great council.

Mariano was the youngest of all the chiefs, and his clan was the smallest. His influence in the council would not probably be felt, and his presence, or his absence, was regarded as a matter of but little importance. Whether present or absent, he would necessarily be governed by the decision of the head chief and the council, whatever it might be; or his people, always true to the traditions of their race, would desert him and join other clans.

From the earliest history of this remarkable people, the tribe had been divided into great families or clans, each governed by its own chief and principal men. The supremacy of a head chief, himself the chief of one of the clans, was acknowledged, and the decisions of the great council, composed of the chiefs and the principal men, were obeyed by virtue of the popular will and the force of traditions.

The chiefs were all men who had distinguished themselves previous to their selection, by their bravery in battle, by the accumulation of large numbers of horses and sheep, and by the wisdom of their counsel. The road to preferment was open to every man of the tribe.

The Navajos possessed great herds and flocks, and were necessarily nomadic. At times, therefore, it happened when a clan had become large, that difficulty was experienced in finding sufficient pasturage for the animals, and separation became a positive necessity. In such case a colony went off under the leadership of some prominent member of the clan.

The success of the enterprise depended largely upon the sagacity and wisdom of the leader. Frequently dissatisfaction arose and open desertions occurred, one after another, until the colony became so reduced in its numbers that the would-be chief was compelled in the end to surrender his honors and return to his clan and his former more humble position. A considerable time, therefore, was allowed to elapse before the chief of a newly organized clan was duly recognized by the head chief, and by common consent.

Mariano had once been the leader of an expedition against the Mescalaro Apaches in the valley of the Tulerosa, and had returned to his tribe with a great herd of horses, and many pack animals ladened with captured blankets and robes. He had gone on this expedition with the consent of the chief of his clan, taking with him a small party of warriors. This unusually successful adventure had attracted the attention of the people, and eventually induced his selection as the leader of a colony. He rapidly thereafter drew about him a number of young men from his former clan, as well as from others, until he stood now at the head of about one hundred braves.

Near the close of a beautiful autumn day, one of the runners despatched by the head chief, arrived at the Rio Puerco, and without stopping to slake the thirst of himself or his horse, galloped furiously down its bank toward the encampment of the young chief. On arriving at the outskirts of the encampment, he dismounted from his horse in token of submission to the authority of the chief into whose jurisdiction he had come, and proceeded on foot, leading his weary beast after him.

As the runner passed the temporary summer houses of the different families of the clan, looking to the right and the left for some sign to guide him to the ho-gan of the chief, a woman, attracted by the tramping of his horse as he passed by her lodge, made her appearance at its entrance. She gazed for a moment at the runner and then in a tone of mingled pleasure and surprise, exclaimed quickly.

"Me-ra! me-ra! It is To-mé. Indeed it is. Welcome, To-mé."

The runner's face lighted up with a smile, but he merely bowed his head in reply. The woman had already started towards him, but as To-mé still continued on his way without giving her any further attention, she stopped and looked after him, greatly perplexed.

"Ah!" she said in a subdued, half-inquiring tone, "It must be that To-mé has words in his mouth for the chief, and cannot speak to Po-lone."

The runner bowed his head and walked steadily on.

"Then To-mé seeks for the ho-gan of Mariano?" asked the woman.

Again the runner nodded his head in reply.

"To-mé must turn his face to the sun for three flights of the longest arrow in his quiver, and then he will find the young chief on the bank of the stream, and then," continued the woman, "when To-mé has done his errand, he must turn quickly back. The fire will soon burn, and ground corn and fresh meat and fine salt will be ready, that To-mé may eat."

The runner again bowed his head, and hastened in the direction indicated by the woman.

The young chief had been aware of the approach of the runner for at least an hour before his arrival. One of his own vigilant warriors had hastened to report that a horseman was "riding rapidly down from the North, straight as the wind blows over the plain, and as a man with the words of the head chief in his mouth."

"He is a runner," said the chief. "Let him alone."

Mariano had received the information with the characteristic indifference of his race, but so soon as the warrior was gone, he sprang to his feet from the robe on which he sat and paced hastily back and forth in front of his ho-gan.

There was nothing remarkable in the personal appearance of the chief, as he thus moved impetuously to and fro. He was tall and slender in form, and lacked the vigorous proportions of limb and of chest, common to his people. But there was something magnetic in his easy, graceful manner, something fascinating in the steady gaze of his brilliant black eyes, and something pleasing in the musical intonations of his voice, that captivated all who came in contact with him.

He had been brave and victorious in battle, successful in the management of his flocks, and his forays, and had proven himself a wise counselor. By these worthy deeds, and his magnetic influence he had won the full confidence and admiration of his people, and now in the prime of his young manhood, he had reached the goal of a warrior's most lofty aspiration, the chieftainship of a clan of his nation.

Mariano possessed a quality, almost entirely unknown among his people. He was inordinately ambitious. From the day when his father had for the first time placed in his hands a strong bow, such as warriors use, and hung a quiver of barbed arrows upon his back he had aspired to excel and to control. No one thereafter, among all his youthful companions, displayed greater daring in the defence of the flocks against the wild beasts from the mountains; and none learned so well how to send the quivering arrow, or hurl the deadly tomahawk and knife.

In savage life, boyhood plays find their origin in stories of the war-path and the chase. Mariano found great delight in these plays, and was never more happy than when, at the head of his companions, engaged in some mimic battle or imaginary chase.

During all the days of his boyhood his leadership was tacitly acknowledged. But when those days were passed, and he had entered upon the real duties of life, he found that his leadership had suddenly ended. The road to royal honors lay open before him, but heavily burdened with traditions and the customs of his people. He found able leaders of great skill and experience already in existence, to manage and control, and himself but an apprentice among the warriors of his clan. He submitted with manifest impatience to this seeming degradation, and rarely accompanied his companions on the war-path or the chase.

In the meantime, however, he never ceased his endeavors to accomplish his preferment. In every instance where individual exertion afforded opportunity, he attempted to excel.

No hunter in the nation ever climbed higher mountains, in following the chase, and none was ever so successful.

No warrior ever spake with more eloquence in the councils of his clan, or bore himself always more courtly.

No one in all the nation possessed richer ornaments, or rode better steed, and no one ever carried more valuable arms.

To these great advantages, was added at last, most notable success in foray and battle. The people hastened then to crown his achievements with the leadership he coveted, and had thus fairly won.

He paced now impatiently back and forth in front of his lodge, gazing earnestly at times in the direction from which the runner was approaching.

"It is well," he murmured slowly, "The great head chief is wise to send a runner to Mariano with a token in his hand."

The runner soon made his appearance, and proceeding directly to the ho-gan of the chief, placed the token in his hand.

"Me-ra!" he said quickly, "To-mé comes from the great council chamber of the nation. The head chief Barbonce-to has spoken."

"To-mé is welcome," said the chief. "The words of the head chief are all good, and Mariano will hasten to the great council chamber, with the principal men of his clan."

"To-mé has no more words in his mouth," said the runner. "His errand is done."

"Then To-mé will loosen his horse on the rich grass a the bank of the river, and return to eat meat in the ho-gan of Mariano."

"Nay," replied the runner. "The woman Po-lone bade To-mé make haste to eat meat and ground corn in her lodge."

"Then To-mé stopped in his journey to talk with a woman," said the chief, haughtily.

"Nay, the woman talked only. To-mé was silent, and stopped not in his journey," replied the runner. "To-mé comes from the great clan of the head chief. No one in the South can teach him what he should do."

"Hist!" exclaimed the chief angrily. "To-mé has the tongue of a squaw in his head. He can go. Mariano has spoken."

The runner gathered his blanket about him, and moved hurriedly away in the direction from which he had come.

He was a tall, athletic fellow, a perfect picture of health and of strength. His features were unusually regular and comely, and his carriage was graceful and erect.

Mariano watched him closely as he walked rapidly away, and then turning about he murmured to himself:

"To-mé is handsome and brave. The woman is not wise to bid him come to her lodge."

The runner proceeded a short distance, and then stopping abruptly, turned towards the lodge of the chief. His manner was defiant and haughty, and his face bore a resolute expression. To-mé was very angry, and in a dangerous mood. His better judgment, however, came directly to his assistance, and turning again in his path he walked on.

"The last words of the young chief are hot," he murmured. "They make a big fire in the ears of To-mé, and burn up all the good words he has spoken."

The woman Po-lone stood at the entrance of her ho-gan, and when he came near, she hastened forward to bid him welcome once more.

"And why does To-mé come now to the Puerco?" asked Po-lone, after they had seated themselves on robes spread on the ground in her lodge.

"To carry a token from the head chief to Mariano, the dog," said the runner savagely, as he suddenly recalled the "hot words" of the chief.

"Me-ra!" cried the woman. "Every thorn on the cactus, and every blade of the grass, has ears that can hear. To-mé must eat his hot words."

"Po-lone speaks wisely," said To-mé.

"And were other runners sent out?" asked the woman.

"Yes, a runner was sent to the chief of every clan of the nation, with a token in his hand. Barbon-ce-to has spoken."

"The words of the head chief are good," said the woman. "Mariano will go up, and take his place in the council among the chiefs of the nation?"

"Yes, the young chief will go up with the principal men of his clan," replied the runner. "Will Po-lone ride with the chief?"

"Yes," she answered quickly. "Po-lone will go up with the chief and hear him talk in the great council."

The runner remained silent.

"To-mé has no words in his mouth?" said the woman, inquiringly.

"Nay," he replied. "The woman spake well, and To-mé has eaten his words."

"Po-lone is wise, sometimes," she said smiling. "Me-ra! To-mé. Po-lone will go up to the council, as one of the principal men of the clan."

She rubbed her hands briskly together, and indulged in a suppressed laugh. To-mé had sat the meanwhile looking gravely at the woman, and nursing his grievance, but her words and her laugh drove his evil thoughts all away, and a broad smile at last crept over his face.

The sun had already gone down behind the tops of the

mountains, and the shadows were rapidly gathering. Within the lodge, the woman and her guest sat almost in darkness. A flickering flame from some dying embers on the fire between them, occasionally cast a feeble light in the lodge, barely sufficient to reveal their motionless forms to each other.

"There is some one at the door," said To-mé, his quick ear catching the faint echo of a footstep.

"Yea," said Po-lone, glancing hastily at the entrance. "It is Nah-nee-ta. She brings sticks for the fire."

"To-mé has heard the birds sing of the beautiful Nah-nee-ta, the daughter of the woman Po-lone," said the runner.

As he spake, the girl moved across the entrance of the lodge, and stood fairly in the faint light yet reflected from the sky. To-mé could see plainly that the birds had sung a true song in his ears. The daughter of Po-lone was beautiful in features and form. Strong, healthful and lithesome, she found favor at once in the eyes of the young man, as his ideal type of womanly perfection.

"Po-lone," cried the girl petulantly, as she entered the lodge, "All the wood has been burned. Not a stick more can be found."

"There is plenty on the mountain," said the mother.

"Yea, but the medicine man will turn the dwarf into a white wolf, if he goes to the mountain."

"Then the brave To-mé will capture him for his robe," said the woman, smiling upon her guest as she spake.

The dwarf was a poor half-witted Mexican captive, whom Po-lone had purchased from his captor a few years before, and now held in peonage. He came into the lodge, and threw down a few pieces of roots and of bark he had gathered, and then sat down upon them to prevent them from being used.

"Che-no will put some sticks on the fire," said the woman, peremptorily. "To-mé must have his supper."

"Eh !" exclaimed the dwarf, springing at once to his feet, and staring fixedly for a moment at the runner, whom he now, for the first time observed.

"To-mé wants his supper," he murmured at last, in a tone of complaint, "and all the wood must be burned."

Taking a few sticks from his precious store, he laid them on the embers in the centre of the lodge. A bright blaze soon sprung up, and quickly revealed the dusky faces of the occupants of the hut.

To-mé sat upright on the robe, and watched the fire as it burned. Occasionally he glanced surreptitiously at the girl who stood near him, the meantime gazing intently in his face. Che-no hastened to her side when he had completed his work, and stared also at the stranger.

"Po-lone has spoken often of the brave runner To-mé," said the girl.

The young warrior glanced hurriedly at her face as she spoke, and then dropping his eyes to the ground, reached down before him and twisted vigorously at the fur of the robe on which he sat, but he made no reply.

" Why do the people call the warrior brave?" persisted the girl. "Is his heart very strong ?"

To-mé twisted more vigorously at the robe than before, but not a word could he find to reply.

" To-mé has no words in his mouth," said the girl despairingly.

"His heart is not strong," added the dwarf. " He wants his supper before he can talk."

To-mé started instantly to his feet, and sprung towards the dwarf. With a great cry of terror Che-no evaded the runner, and fled from the lodge.

"Me-ra! Me-ra!" cried the woman. "The peon has but the half of a head. To-mé must let him alone."

The runner came back and resumed his seat on his robe, while Nah-nee-ta ran out of the hut to look for the dwarf. She came back directly leading the terrified peon by the hand, and shaking her head menacingly at To-mé.

Che-no seated himself near the door, and the girl sat down at length on the robe.

"To-mé will not harm the peon?" she asked.

"Nay," said To-mé, for the first time finding "words in his mouth." "Nay," and then he added in a low tone, "The voice of Nah-nee-ta sounds sweet in the ears of To-mé."

The girl gazed earnestly in his face for an instant as though she feared she had not heard him aright, and then hastily cast her eyes on the ground. They were the first gentle words she ever had heard from the lips of any human being, except possibly from the lips of her mother in her childhood, and they awakened at once in her heart a desire to make a kindly response. But before she could reply, a great confusion came upon her, and she became undecided what to do or to say. She reached forward presently and began to twist at the fur of the robe, while the stout-hearted To-mé employed himself unconsciously the meantime in the same occupation.

The girl finally lifted her eyes from the ground, and glanced at the runner. He had ceased to twist at the robe, and sat gazing in her face, as if waiting for an answer.

"The words of To-mé are all good," she said softly.

The runner reached forward as soon as she had spoken, and seizing her hand, pressed it vigorously in his own.

Such a thing had never before happened in all the history of the nation. There never before had been such a flagrant violation of the known customs of the tribe. The girl was speechless with amazement. Recovering herself almost instantly, however, she shrieked involuntarily, "To-mé!"

"What new trouble is there now?" exclaimed the woman quite sharply, turning around from her work.

The girl rubbed her hands vigorously together and attempted to laugh.

"To-mé will twist all the fur from the robe," she said, "if some one don't stop him."

"Che-no will," said the dwarf, quickly; but the words had no sooner escaped him, than, fearing he had said something again that was wrong, he glanced hurriedly at the young warrior, and then at the door of the lodge, as if to assure himself that the way of escape was still open.

"Che-no need not fear," said the runner, observing the uneasy movements of the dwarf. "His words are all good, and To-mé is his friend."

II

It was fortunate indeed for To-mé that Po-lone had not witnessed the act of affection, nor heard the "soft words" of her guest. Had she done so, her wrath would have known no bounds, and To-mé's reputation as a valiant, strong-hearted warrior would have suffered.

As a people, the Navajos exacted a rigid adherence to all their traditional customs. A demonstration of affection between adults had always been regarded as an indication of weakness, and an acknowledgement of great inferiority. Parents caressed their children in their infancy, and spoke to them in tones of affection, and with words of endearment. But, so soon as the child was able to go to the pastures with the sheep, or to gather sticks for the fire, loving words and affectionate demonstrations all ceased. Affection, doubtless, still existed, but the emotions were controlled and concealed. The common observances of the nation were deemed worthy of first consideration, and invariably took precedence of all acts that affection might prompt.

But a deeper motive than that induced by a blind obedience to the traditions of her people, or by her affection for her child, actuated the woman, and she gladly accepted the observance of these traditions as inevitable, to excuse the act she intended. The customs of the nation had long since established a mother's proprietary right in the person of her maiden daughters, and the privilege to dispose of them by sale, if she desired.

Po-lone often had made mental reckoning of the number of horses, or the broad buttons of silver which the beautiful Nah-nee-ta would bring, to increase the size of her herd, or the number of her ornaments. It was, therefore, simply unpardonable that the honored guest of the lodge, should by any thoughtless act or inconsiderate speech, depreciate the commercial value of the daughter.

But Po-lone, in most blissful ignorance of all that had passed, busied herself with her work, and eventually spread To-mé's supper before him and invited him to eat.

When the runner had devoured the last morsel of the bountiful supply set before him, he turned lazily to the woman, and with an air of satisfaction rubbed his hands slowly together.

"To-mé is happy," he said, languidly.

"And why is To-mé happy?" she asked.

"The meat and the corn was very good," he replied.

"To-mé is easily made happy," said the woman.

"And the heart of the head chief is happy," he continued, abstractedly, as though conversing with himself.

"And why is the heart of the head chief happy?" asked the woman.

"He has always good meat and good corn," said To-mé, "and he has brought a new squaw to his lodge. She was the most beautiful maiden in the clan. He gave two horses for the squaw."

"Two horses!" cried the woman, in a tone of surprise: "Two horses! A choice maiden for two horses! It is impossible!"

"To-mé has but one tongue in his head," said the runner decidedly. "The head chief gave two horses for the squaw."

"Is she strong?" asked the woman, "and willing to work?"

"Yea, strong," replied To-mé, " and always willing to work. No squaw in the nation knows better than she how to cook meat and corn. The head chief will have no other squaw now, to smooth out his robe or saddle his horse."

"Me-ra!" exclaimed Po-lone, earnestly. "The head chief did not give enough for the maiden."

"Two horses are enough for a maiden," said To-mé."

"Nay, not enough," said the woman. "Nah-nee-ta shall never go for two horses."

"She might go for none," said To-mé.

"Go for none!" cried the woman excitedly. "The words of To-mé are like the words of a dream. Is To-mé awake?"

"Yea, To-mé is awake," he replied, "and his words are all good. To-mé is too young yet to dream. The Great Spirit whispers only in the ears of the old men while they sleep."

"He once whispered some words in the ear of poor Che-no," said the dwarf.

"Tonto!" cried the girl, "keep quiet. It was nothing but a bug, that buzzed in the ear of the peon."

"He spake once to an old man in the clan of the head chief," continued To-mè, "while he lay quietly sleeping on his robes."

"And what words did the Great Spirit speak in the ears of the old man?" asked the woman.

"The Great Spirit came to his lodge, and whispered in his ears," said To-mé, "and the old man awakened and listened, and waited, until the Great Spirit had gone. Then evil spirits came quickly, and tried to whisper new words in his ears and tried to steal the good words away, the Great Spirit had spoken. But the old man would not listen to the words of the evil spirits. He got up from his robes, and put sticks on his fire, and made a great light, to drive the evil spirits away. All night long the old man walked about in his ho-gan, and never lay down, nor slept any more until the sun was up high above the plain. Then he went out of his lodge, and called his people about him, and told them the words that the Great Spirit had spoken.

" The medicine men of the clan, came quickly to his lodge, and beat on their drums, chanted good words while he talked, and kept the evil spirits away. When the old man had spoken, the people went away to their ho-gans, and he lay down again on his robe and soon fell asleep.

" The medicine men sat down in his lodge, and put sticks on the fire, and made a great light, and beat on their drums, and chanted good words, all the night long. And when the second day came, the same words were in the mouth of the old man that he had spoken at first. And he lay down again on his robes, when the night had come on, and slept while the medicine men kept the evil spirits away. And on the third day, the old man again spoke, and the words in his mouth were the same as before.

" And after a time the old man sickened and died, and was burned in his lodge, and the words that the Great Spirit had whispered in his ears were soon forgotten by the people. But the wise medicine men treasured them up in their hearts, and have remembered them all."

"Have the medicine men spoken to To-mé?" inquired the woman.

"The medicine men have few words in their mouths," said To-mé, "except for those who place buttons of silver in their hands, or horses in their herds."

"Then why has To-mé spoken of them?"

"Po-lone is impatient," said the runner. "To-mé once saved the life of a great medicine man, and asked no reward. Then the medicine man found words in his mouth, and spake to To-mé. He said not that the words which he spake were the words of the Great Spirit, or that they were his own. Who knows? They are from the mouth of a medicine man, and they are every one good.

" 'The Navajo Nation is a great nation,' he said, 'the

people are happy and have large flocks of sheep and great
herds of horses. The medicine men are wise, and have
heard the words which the Great Spirit has spoken. The
Navajos came from a small thing at first, but now they
have grown very great. Let all the people listen to the
words of the medicine men.

"'The rain fell on the land, and filled all the valleys with
water, even to the tops of the mountains. On the highest
peak sat the only living thing. A turkey sat on the top of
the mountain. Then the waters disappeared and the turkey
was alone.

"'The Great Spirit came down on the mountain, and saw
the great desolation. Then the Great Spirit was sorry, and
He changed the turkey into the form of a man. And because
of His sorrow, He made the man perfect. He was pleased
with His work and called the man Navajo—the best. The
turkey is sacred. Let him live on the mountains in peace.

"'The Great Spirit sent a woman to the man. Their
children fill the valleys, and are rich.'

"Then the medicine man cast his eyes on the ground and
was silent."

"It may be that he was hungry," said the the dwarf.

"Tonto!" cried the girl, stamping her foot angrily on the
ground." "Will the fool never be quiet?"

"The medicine man remained silent for a long time,"
continued To-mé, "and his head was bowed down near the
earth. At last he looked up, and spake once again.

"'The Navajos have many customs,' he said, 'and they
are all very good, save one. They were made for the Navajos
and suit all their wants. They are like moccasins made for
the feet of a youth. They hold his feet tight, when he has
grown to be old.

"'One custom has come into the nation from its enemies.
It is not good.

'It is not good that maidens should be sold. It is not good that a warrior should buy a squaw. The children of a bought-woman are fatherless. The squaws become mothers for a price.'

" The medicine man again bowed his head and was silent. There were no more words in his mouth."

The runner turned to the woman when he had concluded, and quietly said:

" Were not the words of the medicine man good ?"

" Yea, the words of the medicine man were all good," she replied.

" Po-lone will hearken to the words of the medicine man?" he asked.

" The customs of the Nation bind every one, with thongs which cannot be broken," said Po-lone. "Come they from evil or from good, maidens must be sold, and the warriors must buy them." And then she added testily, as if to reassert her authority, which she feared the words of To-mé had tended somewhat to weaken, " Nah-nee-ta will go to her robes."

The dwarf immediately recognized the ill mood of his mistress, and hastily spreading a sheep skin across the entrance to the lodge, waited not for a bidding, but lay down quickly, and covered himself with a blanket.

The girl went slowly to a corner of the lodge, and lay down on her bed.

To-mé himself, chilled to silence by the manner of his hostess, speedily stretched himself upon the robe on which he sat, and turning his face from the fire, covered himself with his blanket.

Perfect silence now reigned in the lodge, and all its inmates, except Po-lone, were soon lost in deep slumber.

The period is by no means yet remote, when the account

of the origin of the Navajo Nation, as narrated by the young warrior, would have been received with far greater incredulity than at present. Public opinion has undergone something of a change in many respects, within the memory of the living, and among other things it has learned gradually to tolerate, if not indeed to respect, opinions that differ from those commonly accepted as true.

Although firm adherents in the belief that the whole human family sprung originally from one common head, the American people would now scarcely be angry, but simply amused at the credulity of the savage who taught that his people had origin in a separate creation. They would class him, good humoredly, doubtless, as a follower of Morton and Gliddon, and a believer in the doctrine of the primeval diversity of man.

But who can say, after all, when intelligent research has been made, that the views of Morton and Gliddon, and the untutored savage as well, are improbable?

At least, no one can say that they are impossible, for that would imply a limit to the powers of the Great First Cause, and would impair the belief in His omnipotence.

Neither can any one say that the creation of man, in his second estate, as well as in his first, was impossible; for that, if shown to be true, would destroy the perfection of Deity.

If, then, the primeval diversity of mankind is by no means impossible, why should we regard it as improbable, since such vast differences are clearly apparent between the great sub-divisions of the race?

Guided alone by our reason, we would most certainly agree that the great fund of knowledge now at command indicates almost conclusively the separate creation of the various races of men.

Bishop Butler, in the introduction to his "Analogy," informs us that "probability is the most reliable of all guides in life." If, therefore, this view of the origin of the races can be admitted as probable, it makes a safe guide for the settlement of a much discussed question, and gives peace and a delightful solution to many things that now appear totally irreconcilable. As Morton himself more happily puts it, it gives us "a theory to explain the otherwise unintelligible phenomena, so remarkably stamped on the races of men."

But, unfortunately, public opinion, to which we are compelled to defer, has determined that the whole human family sprung from one common source, and adheres persistently to its faith, notwithstanding Morton and Gliddon and the apparent teachings of nature. Necessarily, therefore, accepting the popular theory as the true one, let us take Bishop Butler's suggestion, and endeavor to determine briefly the probabilities of the origin of the people of our story.

At a remote and uncertain period in the past history of the world, wandering fugitives, hard pressed by their enemies, or daring adventurers fulfilling destiny, pushed their way Eastward from Northern Asia, and eventually found homes in America.

Little better mentally, no doubt, than the wild beasts with which they contended for the possession of the inhospitable region to which they had come, they lived on for ages, slowly pushing their way Southward as their numbers increased, and hanging on tenaciously to the habits and the speech of their ancestors. Behind them in the land of their fathers, the same language and customs existed the meanwhile, unchanged. Held fast in the embrace of dense ignorance and stupidity, this silent witness of the migration, transmitted from one generation to another almost unimpaired, still re-

mains among the Esquimaux of America, and the Tchuk-
tches of Asia, to indicate their common origin.

Within the same period, doubtless, there came here and
there to the Western coast of America, drifting junks with
Japanese crews, bearing involuntary emigrants, destined under the providence of the Almighty, to people the New
World.

Occasionally, too, there came helpless vessels from Europe,
drifting with the Eastern trades to total destruction in the
end, upon the rough coast of the Atlantic. So drifted the
unconscious Portugese to the shores of Brazil, on their first
voyage to India. And so, often, even now, with all the aids
to navigation which modern civilization has given, helpless
crafts from one cause or another, drift from their course
and perish at last upon some unfriendly shore.

From these involuntary emigrants, and the roving bands
that now and then pushed across from Northern Asia, and
thence found their way Southward as far as the chain of the
great lakes, came the aborigines of America.

As their numbers increased, and generations succeeded,
the influences of the climate and the new life of the people,
gradually produced changes in ther habits and appearance.
Dependent upon the chase for their food, they grew wild and
restless like the beasts which they pursued. Familiar with
danger, they became self-reliant aud brave.

At first, doubtless, they adopted some strict forms of
government for the protection of the rights of individuals,
and for the control of the vicious. But the restraints thus
imposed soon became burdensome, as the new character
developed, and were at last entirely abandoned for more
primitive methods.

A boundless country lay about them, covered with dense
forests filled with wild game, and traversed by wide rivers,

abounding in fish. At times vines were discovered bearing rich fruits, and trees ladened with nuts. Tempted thus to become wanderers, they pushed slowly on into the unknown regions around them, to the East and the West and the South.

Here and there, small colonies moved on together, confirmed in their wanderings, or in search of more desirable locations for their homes, until at last, widely separated by great forests and rivers they became totally distinct in their habits and customs, and in time strangers to each other.

Sometimes, vicious individuals fled from the vengeance of outraged communities, and established themselves anew beyond the limit of pursuit. About them, in time, new communities grew into existence, bearing often the evil traits of their founders.

Spreading out thus, slowly but surely, moulded by the peculiar circumstances that surrounded each community and its ever-growing sub-divisions, the great Indian tribes found their birth. The traditions of their origin died slowly away, and were supplanted at last by a belief in a separate and distinct creation of the original progenitors of their people.

The woman sat near the fire holding her head with her hands, evidently in deep thought, and much troubled. Her plans for the future had been unexpectedly endangered, and she was in great doubt what course to pursue. Many hopeful solutions presented themselves to her mind, but so soon as she had reasoned each one out to its probable conclus'' some other would appear that seemed better. Many long, weary hours passed away and she still sat thinking and perplexed.

She had good reason to expect that the great beauty of Nah-nee-ta would attract the attention of the young chief and other rich warriors of the nation, and that there would be much competition, and many offers made for her. She knew that To-mé did not possess horses enough to enable him to bid with any show of success, and she had believed that he would have the good sense to recognize this fact, and would make no offers. Should he bid higher than his competitors would be likely to bid, he would utterly impoverish himself, and take the girl home to a destitute lodge.

Po-lone wished to avoid such a result. Indeed she had decided upon a different course for To-mé, and it now troubled her greatly that he could not see what it was without being told. When the girl had been disposed of, and she was left alone in her lodge, she had determined to propose to To-mé that he should " turn his horses in her herd," and share her lodge with her thereafter.

This business method of acquiring a husband, was common in the nation among unmarried widows, and many young warriors would have gladly received an invitation from the woman, to " turn their horses in her herd," and share her wealth with her thereafter.

Po-lone was well satisfied from the language which To-mé had used, that his heart was now set on buying the girl, and that he would bid boldly for her. The question she wished, therefore, at once to decide, was how to prevent him from pursuing such a course. One plan after another presented itself, and each in its turn was rejected. She had never before been so sorely perplexed to determine what she should do.

She arose at last to her feet, and groped about in the darkness, until she found the few remaining pieces of bark and of roots, that the dwarf had collected, and gathering these in her arms, she brought them to the center of the lodge, and laid them carefully one by one, on the live coals which yet remained, and again sat down in her place.

To-mé moved about uneasily in his blanket. The footsteps of the woman had disturbed him, and although scarcely awake, he was conscious that some one was moving about in the lodge. In an instant, the force of long established habit reasserted itself, and he sat up quickly on his robe, and looked about him. His eyes fell directly on the woman sitting wide awake near the fire. It occurred to him at once, that Po-lone had been disturbed by the noise, and he felt no little annoyance to think that a squaw had exceeded him in vigilance. For a time he sat quietly looking about him without saying a word.

"Did Po-lone bring wood for the fire?" he asked her at length.

"Yes," she replied.

"Footsteps drive sleep from the eyes of To-mé."

"Yea," said the woman, "but can To-mé tell what drives sleep from the eyes of Po-lone?"

"No; To-mé cannot tell. Has Po-lone not slept?"

"No; Po-lone cannot sleep."

Ah! thought To-mé, the words of the medicine man have sunk deep into her ears, and have driven out the horses that were there, as the price of the beautiful Nah-nee-ta. To-mé will make the woman happy by a gift, and the girl shall go to his lodge.

"Po-lone," he said at length, somewhat desperately, "the words of the medicine man were good."

"They were all very good," she said solemnly.

"Po-lone shall choose two of the best horses in the herd of To-mé for her own, and Nah-nee-ta shall go to his lodge."

"Nay, two horses are not enough."

"Three then."

"Hark now," said the woman, "how many horses has To-mé in his herd?"

"Five only. Po-lone must be reasonable."

"To-mé must be wise, and not make himself a beggar for a squaw. Nay, To-mé," she continued after a brief pause, "leave the horses in the herd, and when the great council is over, drive them all to the South, and turn them loose in the herd of Po-lone."

To-mé was speechless with surprise. The proposition of the woman was so entirely unexpected, that he could scarcely believe what he heard. Po-lone was yet young, and good-looking withal, and the offer she made was a most desirable one. Before Nah-nee-ta had crossed his path, the young warrior would have been glad to accept it. But now he had set his heart on the daughter, what could he say to the mother? If he rejected her offer, he would incur her bitter enmity, and destroy forever all hope of obtaining possession of the beautiful Nah-nee-ta. What should he say? To-mé was sadly perplexed and bowed down his head, and covered his face with his hands, like one lost in thought. At last he raised up his head and uncovered his face. The woman sat silently watching him, and waiting for an answer.

"The words of Po-lone are all good," he said at length, submissively.

"To-mé is wise. He is good, and he is brave," said the woman softly, her voice scarcely rising above a whisper. "Hearken well now to the words of Po-lone. The beautiful Nah-nee-ta is a Mexican."

"A Mexican!" exclaimed To-mé, contemptuously.

"Yea, a Mexican, born is a casa of the vile, hated race, on the bank of the great river, the Rio Grande del Norte."

"And she is not the daughter of Po-lone?"

"Yea, she is the daughter of Po-lone, and the master of Po-lone was her father."

"Were there no warriors to buy Po-lone when she was a girl?" asked To-mé indignantly.

"There were no warriors to defend Po-lone when she was a girl," said the woman sadly, "or the Mexicans would never have been able to steal her as they did from the midst of the Nation."

"To-mé's face burns with shame at the words of the woman."

"Nay, it was not because the warriors were not brave, but because they were few. The Mexicans were strong, and came in great haste by mountain trails seldom used. When their approach was discovered the runners of the head chief rode rapidly about to spread the alarm, and warn the people to flee. Beacon fires were lighted in haste on the mountains, that all the nation might be speedily aroused.

"The Mexicans rode rapidly up the great valley, leading to the North from the cañon Bo-neet. While they moved in the middle of the valley, the smoke from the fires went up from the mountains on the East and the West. When they moved from one side or the other, a great column of smoke could be seen on that side alone. As they advanced up the valley the columns of smoke advanced with them, and rose up one after another, further and further to the North.

"A portion of the clan of the head chief lived in the valley at the time, and was in an almost defenseless condition. Nearly all the young warriors of the clan had been called away by the great war chief Manuloto, and had gone on the war path against the Apaches.

"The women and the children and the old men fled to the mountains in the greatest consternation. The Mexicans dashed upon them before they could reach places of safety, and, seizing the women and children, permitted the others to escape. Then gathering the scattered herds of horses together as rapidly as possible they rode furiously back to the

South by the way they had come, carrying their captives with them.

"The plain resounded with the shrieks and the cries of the women and children, the rushing of the horses and the loud shouts of the Mexicans. The women did not submit tamely, but struggled and fought like wounded wild beasts with the hunters. Many escaped from their captors and fled towards the mountains, evading pursuit among the rocks of the foot-hills, and finally got safely away."

The woman spoke slowly and earnestly in the meagre tongue of her people, helping out often the half hidden purport of her words, with idiomatic expressions and gestures, with which her companion was familiar. With sighs and with groans and with many vigorous gestures that baffle description, and with broken speech that makes literal rendition impossible, she proceeded with her story.

"In the meantime," she continued, "a number of warriors had hastily gathered, and were waiting in concealment at a point in the valley but a short distance from the place where the Mexicans had ceased to advance. When the warriors discovered that their enemies were leaving the valley, they quickly mounted their horses and followed at once in pursuit.

"The Mexicans almost immediately abandoned the horses they had taken, and defended themselves with their arms. They fought very bravely until night had set in, when they fled down the valley under cover of darkness.

"All the women who had been captured, were either rescued by the warriors, or succeeded in effecting their escape, except only Po-lone, and she too would have made good her escape, and have reached a safe place with the others, but for a false step which she made as she ran. She fell heavily to the ground, and her head striking a stone that lay in her path, she became quickly unconscious. When she recovered her thoughts, she found herself in the arms of her captor riding rapidly to the South.

" The Mexican rode a powerful, black horse, of wonderful speed and endurance, and was soon well in advance of his companions. Finally when it became dark, he abandoned them entirely, and pushed his way Southward, alone with his captive. About midnight he halted and dismounted to permit the animal to rest. The noise of the tramping of the horses, and the voices of the Mexicans calling to each other, as they galloped down the valley in the darkness, had gradually died away in the distance, and now could no longer be heard. The occasional wailing cry of a coyote, alone broke the great silence of the night.

" At daylight on the following morning the Mexican reached the country of the Aqua Azul, and again halted to give his weary horse a few moments to rest. The great speed which had been kept up during all the previous night, had fatigued the noble animal, and his master anxiously watched him as he slowly cropped the short grass on the bank of the stream.

"The Mexican knew that rapid pursuit would be made, and that it would be pushed to the very hills that overlook the valley of the Rio Grande. He was therefore anxious to move forward as rapidly as the condition of his horse would permit. The main body of the Mexicans was still behind him, and he hoped it was yet between him and his pursuers. But the warriors rode hardy horses, accustomed to long, rapid journeys, and he feared that they might possibly have passed his companions during the night, or have pushed across the mountains, by trails known only to themselves, in order to reach some point in the valley, when they would be able to intercept his retreat, with the advantage of position.

Such a point he knew existed, some miles yet below in the valley, and his safety might depend upon reaching it first.

"He started on presently again, this time walking briskly along on the trail, leading his horse after him, and driving his captive before. After walking some time, he reached a low range of hills over which the trail lay, and ascended to its top. From this point he could see a great distance up the valley, in the direction from which he had come. A body of horsemen were in view galloping rapidly towards him. The Mexican shaded his eyes with his hand, and watched them anxiously for awhile. He was evidently unable to determine whether they were his comrades following after, or the dreaded warriors in pursuit. At last, acting upon his fears, he hastily mounted his horse, and taking his captive up quickly behind him, galloped on furiously again. After a few hours hard riding, he came within sight of a narrow opening through the Mal Pais. This was the place which he feared his pursuers might have reached, and as he approached nearer, he rode back and forth across the narrow valley, looking attentively on the ground for foot marks of horses and men. He soon became convinced that the warriors had not reached the pass, and riding slowly forward, he cautiously advanced by the narrow opening, into the dreaded evil land.

"From the base of steep mountains on the right and on the left of the pass, the whole valley was filled with a rough, broken mass of black lava. Great fissures yawned between these broken masses so deep down in the earth, that the darkness never left them. Hope died in Po-lone's heart when she found that the warriors had not reached the pass, and she wept, and struggled hard to escape.

"Finally, loosing herself from the grasp of the Mexican, she sprang to the ground and fled back along the pass for

some distance, and then attempted to conceal herself between the great broken masses of lava. She shrank back
in terror from each opening that she attempted to enter.
They were all dark, bottomless houses of evil things, waiting to close up forever some poor human being.

"The Mexican was soon in pursuit, and, directly overtaking
his captive, seized her by the hair, and threw her with great
force to the ground. Then fastening the end of his lariat
about one of her ankles, he returned to his horse, dragging
his captive behind him, over the rough ground.

III.

To-mé had sat the meanwhile listening attentively to the story of the woman, but exhibiting no evidence of the great indignation and the burning desire for revenge, which her words had awakened. But he could now no longer conceal his emotion, and rising quickly from the robe on which he sat, he suddenly drew his hunting knife from its sheath, and threw it violently to the ground.

"Why should the warriors of the Nation have weapons?" he cried, indignantly. "They are squaws, every one, and weapons are useless in their hands. Nay," he said hurriedly, again grasping his knife. "To-mé will go, even now, to the great river, and bring back to Po-lone the scalp of the Mexican."

"Nay, brave To-mé, wait a breath only. The journey would be useless."

"Po-lone shall speak on," he said, and after a brief hesitation, again seated himself on the robe.

"The girl finally got up on her feet," said Po-lone, once more continuing her story, "and followed her captor submissively. Mounting his horse now again, he took her up quickly behind him, and fastening the lariat to his saddle, rode rapidly forward.

"The terrible Mal Pais extended for a long, long distance, and the dark graves in the way lay close to the pass, and yawned threateningly at the Mexican and his captive. Po-lone's heart grew faint at the sight of the graves, and she closed both her eyes and held fast to her captor. She had no more desire to escape, not even from the cruel fetters that bound her. She was glad that her foot was tied fast to the saddle, and that the lariat was strong and could not be broken. She forgot the pain of her bruises in the great terror that now filled her heart, and thought no more of her great hatred for her captor.

"At last the southern entrance of the pass into the terrible Mal Pais was reached, and the Mexican rode down into a beautiful valley, along the clear waters of the Gio. From this point he made frequent halts, to permit his horse to take needed rest and to graze, and often walked on in silence, leading the weary beast after him, and driving the captive before. At last the sun disappeared behind the mountains, and the darkness again fell upon the earth.

"The trail had left the valley when the sun was far down and now wound tortuously over a broken mountain range, that lay between the Gio and the valley of the Rio Grande. The weary horse, no longer able to carry his burden, followed after his master with slow and faltering steps. The terrible night dragged' slowly on, and the poor exhausted captive, al most unable to proceed, sank often to the ground and quickly fell asleep amid the threats and the blows of her captor. Sometimes he let her sleep for a while, that his weary horse might have rest, but often raised her up roughly and forced her to go on again.

"At last the soft, gray light of the early morning fell gently from the sky, and rested like a dream upon the earth. The Mexican had now reached the summit of the mountain, and had halted to await the coming of the light. It came slowly on, gradually bringing into view a great valley, through which a wide river ran, and at last revealed a little village, half hidden among some trees, that grew upon the banks of the stream. The Mexican gave a great shout for joy, and the horse raised up his head and neighed, as though he, too, recognized, as well as his master, that his journey was near its end.

"The Mexican was received by his people with caresses, and with many kind words of welcome ; but for the poor captive there were only looks of great hatred, and fierce glances from dark, burning eyes. In a short time she was hurried with rough gestures to the kitchen, where, one after another, all the people in the casa, came directly to stare at her, as though she was a wild beast from the mountains. After she had eaten some food, a merciful sleep came upon her, and for a long time poor Po-lone forgot all her troubles.

"The mistress of the casa hated the Indian girl from the first, and treated her always most cruelly. No one dared show any pity for the poor captive, without provoking hot words from the mistress. The master himself got his full share from her long busy tongue, and there was no peace in the casa.

"At last a great medicine man, whom the Mexicans called padre, came to the casa. The master and the mistress received him, with all the honor due to a chief, and, with many kind words, bade him welcome.

"But the padre's face was much troubled, and he found but few words in his mouth to reply.

"'The people talk,' he said solemnly. 'They say there is no peace in the casa. Is what they say true?'

"'Nay,' said the master, 'the people like much to talk, and—'

"'Let the mistress speak first,' said the padre.

"The mistress hung down her head, as if in doubt what to say. At last she found courage to answer :

"'There is an Indian captive in the casa, dear padre,' she said, 'and she does not know good things from vile. There can be no peace while the captive is here.'

"'Then send her away,' said the padre.

"'Alas ! dear padre, the master will not.'

"'She must go,' said the padre, decidedly. 'There must be peace in the casa.'

"'Shall she be set free in the mountains?' asked the mistress. 'She could find her way back to her people.'

"'Nay, that would be cruel.'

"'She could have her blankets and some food?' urged the mistress.

"'Nay,. I tell thee,' said the padre, quite hotly. 'The saints forbid that such a cruel thing should be done.' And then, after a long silence, he added softly: 'She may come to the casa of the padre, until some other home can be found for her.'

"The words of the padre were not welcome in the ears of the master, but he dared not disobey, and calling a peon, he bade him saddle a horse and take the captive up behind him and follow the padre. The mistress found many words in her mouth, as the captive rode away, for the dear padre, who had brought peace to the casa, but the master uncovered his head, and looked on in silence.

"There were many wonderful things, To-mé, in the ho-gan of the padre. Queer-shaped pieces of wood, and twisted grass, tied together, were used by the people for seats. A great beautiful blanket lay upon the ground, and covered it completely from sight. A curious thing called a table, stood in the room, and pictures of men and of animals, hung on the walls.

"But one thing, To-mé, was the most wonderful of all. It was a great, bright, shining shield, made of silver, held fast in its place on the wall, by small pieces of wood fastened together about it. When one looked ·in the shield, a face could be seen. It was the spirit of the one who stood before it and looked. It was much like the spirit of one who looks down into deep, clear water. But the spirit in the water is weak. The spirit in the shining shield of the padre, is strong.

"A few pieces of wood burned brightly on the fire, and the casa was well lighted by the blaze. But the padre was not pleased with the light. He took up a stick that lay on the table, and rubbed it hard on the wall, and fire came out from the wall, and set the stick in a blaze. Then he touched the blaze to a string of twisted wool, in the center of a long piece of tallow, and it burned slowly, and gave a great light in the casa. At last the padre took a small bell from the table and rang it. A woman soon came to the door, and after the padre had spoken, she beckoned Po-lone to follow her, and went quickly away.

"For a time the woman had hot words in her mouth for Po-lone, but she soon found that the captive was strong, and willing to work, and her heart grew soft and her words became kind. Then each day she spent a long time in teaching the girl something useful and strange.

"There was a dwarf in the casa," she continued, nodding her head toward Cheno, as she spake, "and his heart, too, was soft, and his words were all kind.

"Many moons passed away and the time came at last when the captive was welcome no more in the casa of the padre.

"One day he found words in his mouth, and calling Po-lone to him put his hands on her head and bade her go back to the casa of the Mexican.

"Poor Po-lone was very sad when she heard the words of the padre, and her heart sank within her. She fell on the ground and wet his feet with her tears, and begged that he would not send her away.

"'Nay,' said the padre, 'Po-lone must go now. It may be that at some other time, she can come. It is not proper now that she should be here.'

"So the poor girl was sent back to the casa of the Mexican, and took her old place in the kitchen.

"At last her baby was born and the grief of Po-lone was turned into joy.

"One moon after another now passed quickly away, and the child grew in strength and in beauty. But the mistress hated the mother and the child, and there was no peace in the casa. In her anger, one day, she struck at the child with her hand.

" 'Coyote !' screamed Po-lone, frantic with rage, 'Coyote ! and dog,' and seizing a stick that lay near the fire, she gave the mistress a blow on her head that felled her to the ground. Then seizing her child and her blanket, she fled from the casa.

"Once outside the walls she stopped, almost in the door, undecided what next she should do. Her poor thoughts were all at war with each other. Her first impulse was to flee down the river to the casa of the padre. But it flashed quick on her mind that he might not receive her. Then she would flee to the mountains and attempt to escape to her people. But no, the master would follow and overtake her before the mountains could be reached. There was nothing left for her to do after all, but to fly to the casa of the padre, and beg his protection and trust to his kindness.

"Gathering her babe closer in her arms she hurried away. She had only taken a few steps, when, raising her eyes, she observed several people coming along the great trail not far from the casa. If she should continue her flight they would, doubtless, soon stop her, and compel her to return. She stopped short in the path, and turning about walked slow back, not knowing what else to do.

"Suddenly her eyes fell upon the horse of the Mexican, the same noble black horse, that had carried her into captivity, standing quietly at the door of the corral, ready saddled and bridled for the use of his master. Running at once to his side, she sprang into the saddle and galloped away towards the mountains.

"After riding some time she turned in her saddle, and looked back at the casa. She was much surprised to observe that she was already pursued. The master and two of his peons, had hastily mounted and were riding rapidly in pursuit. She urged her horse to greater speed than before, and rode boldly for the nearest foot-hills, following a trail made by the carrettas that went daily to the mountains for wood.

"At last the trail ceased entirely, and the mountain became steep and difficult to climb. The horse moved forward slowly, picking his steps among the loose stones in the way. He had gotten well to the top, when he suddenly stopped, and, raising his head, looked intently before him in the bushes. Then turning quickly about he attempted to run back by the way he had come.

" Po-lone found it almost impossible to force him to turn and move on up the mountain again. In her fear and excitement she shouted to him in the Navajo tongue, and promised him rest for all of his days, if he would bear her in safety to her people again. But the horse was greatly alarmed, and could scarcely be made to go forward at all. She succeeded, however, in forcing him on, and had almost reached the top of the mountain, when three warriors sprung suddenly out from the cover of bushes before her. One instantly cast a long lasso about the neck of the horse, and quickly led him aside.

" A single glance at the warriors made the heart of Po-lone jump quick for joy. One was a Navajo, and the two others were Utes.

"' A woman from the nation!' cried the Navajo hurriedly.

"'Yes,' answered Po-lone, 'a captive from the nation fleeing from her master. The pursuers are already in sight.'

"The warriors led the horse quickly behind some rocks to conceal him, and bade Po-lone hasten to hide in the bushes.

"The horse pawed the ground as his master approached, and struggled to break the rope with which he was tied. At last he raised up his head and neighed loudly. The pursuers were but a short distance away, and they gave a great shout in answer to the call of the horse, and almost immediately after they came in full view, riding up the side of the mountain. At the instant they made their appearance, the sharp twang of three bow strings sounded clear in the air and three barbed arrows sped swiftly away.

"The Mexican reeled for an instant in his saddle, and then fell dead to the ground. One of the peons fell almost by the side of his master, and the other, sorely wounded, at once made his escape, and rode rapidly away down the mountain. The warriors soon succeeded in capturing the horses which the Mexican and the peon had ridden, and anticipating immediate pursuit, set out in great haste for the North.

"The Navajo belonged to one of the great clans of the nation, living on the border of the country of the Utes, and the trail of the party lay far from the valley where the family of Po-lone built their ho-gans, and pastured their flocks. After many days of hard riding the warriors reached the country of the Utes. Here the Navajo and his companions divided the horses and the arms they had captured, and separated, the Utes going farther on to the North to return to their people, and the Navajo turning to the South in search of his ho-gan.

"To-pa-ha was kind to Po-lone, and his words were all good, and she went with him at last to live in his lodge. Many moons came and went, and To-pa-ha and his squaw lived in great peace. But at last poor To-pa-ha lay sick in his ho-gan. The medicine men came and chanted their songs, and beat on their drums and made great fires, to drive the evil spirits away. But the evil work had been done, even before they had come, and all their efforts proved useless to save him. When he was dead the body was laid in the center of the lodge, and after the days of mourning were over, it was burned where it lay.

"Po-lone started then to the South in search of her people, driving before her the flocks and the herds that had belonged to her husband. Once or more she had sent a message to her people that she had been rescued from the Mexicans, and was living with her husband in the North. When she arrived at the ho-gan of her mother, her heart was made glad by the words of praise that she heard for the brave To-pa-ha, who had rescued her from the Mexicans on the night of her capture, and had carried her away to his ho-gan in the North. Po-lone kept her words in her mouth, and Nah-nee-ta is known in the nation, as To-pa-ha's daughter."

When the woman had finished her story, she bowed down her head, and covered her face with her hands. A long silence ensued, unbroken save by the heavy breathing of the sleeping girl and the dwarf. At last the woman raised up her head, and drawing her blanket about her arose to her feet, and going to the corner of the lodge, lay down by the side of her daughter. When she had gone, To-mé again stretched himself slowly upon his robe, and was soon fast asleep.

IV.

The people of the village were moving about at an early hour in the morning, and To-mé was speedily awakened by the tramping of feet, mingled with the cries of the peons and squaws who were gathering together the herds and the flocks of the several families of the clan, to drive them to the pastures along the banks of the stream.

To-mé sprang to his feet, and, drawing his blanket about him, passed out of the lodge.

The sun was just rising above the summit of the mountains, gilding the encampment with his first golden rays. To the Eastward, in the valley along the banks of the stream, dark shadows yet lingered, almost obstructing the view. Far away to the Westward, the mountain tops seemed ablaze with the light, and all the rock-covered peaks were crested with great burning crowns.

To-mé gazed about him in silence for awhile, and then turning his face to the East, looked intently at the sun.

"What has To-mé in his eyes?" cried a voice near him.

"To-mé's heart is made glad," he replied, without removing his gaze. "The light of the Great Spirit has come once again, to drive the evil shadows from the land of the Nation. The Great Spirit is good."

"And the light will drive the evil shadows from the trail of the young chief, and the principal men of the clan as they ride."

"Yes."

"Does To-mé ride with them?"

"Where do they ride?"

"To the great council chamber."

"No! To-mé will not ride."

"Will not To-mé ride with the chief?"

Indignant that the question had been asked him again, To-mé was about to make an angry reply, but he suddenly recalled the words of the woman, that she would accompany the young chief to the council, and after a short pause he said quietly.

"Yes, To-mé will ride."

"Has To-mé two tongues in his head?"

"Nay, To-mé has but one tongue in his head," he replied sharply, "but his thoughts were at war. They are all now at peace; To-mé will ride with the chief."

"To-mé is wise. It is best to forget the hot words of a brother, and live always in peace."

The runner turned instantly about, and looked at the speaker. The young chief stood before him, his face bearing a smile, and his hand extended for a greeting. To-mé's face instantly grew dark, and his eyes burned like live coals of fire. Stepping back for a pace he drew his blanket more closely about him, and refused to notice the extended hand of the chief.

"Nay, brave To-mé, let there be peace. The words of Mariano were hot, and his heart now is sad. Mariano is the friend of every warrior in the nation. Why should he think evil of the bravest of them all? To-mé will yet be a great chief among his people, and his example must be good. Let the light of the Great Spirit drive the shadows from his heart, even as it has driven them now from the valley."

"The words of the chief are all good," said To-mé, and stepping forward with some hesitation, he took the hand of the young chief in his own. It was motionless and cold, and chilled him to his heart. He dropped it at once, and looked the chief earnestly in the face, as though he sought to find there some evidence of deceit. But the face of Mariano still wore the same quiet smile, and his eyes shone kindly, as he returned the fixed gaze of the runner.

But the doubts of To-mé were by no means removed. The matter between them had been formally adjusted, but he felt that at heart the grievance of both still existed. There was no alternative, however. He had given his hand, and by the precedent of custom, he could never recall his past grievance.

"When will Mariano and his warriors ride?" he asked at length, in as quiet a tone as he was able to command.

"When the shadows measure the height of the lodges on the ground. Even now, the runners are gone to bid those who will go."

"The words of the chief are all good," said To-mé, and turning about, he walked slowly away towards the lodge of the woman.

The dwarf had already returned from a search for more fuel, bringing an armful of roots and of sticks, and Po-lone was busily engaged in preparing some food for her guest.

"The chief rides to-day, to the North," said To-mé, as he entered the lodge. "Have his runners bidden Po-lone?"

"Nay," said the woman, "the runners have passed the lodge often, but they had no words in their mouths for Po-lone."

"Then Po-lone cannot go."

"Hark, now, To-mé, Po-lone rides a horse well."

"Yea, but no squaw in the nation knows better the customs of the tribe, than Po-lone," said To-mé, smiling quietly as he spake. "They bind one with thongs which cannot be broken. No one rides with the chief of a clan, unless specially bidden."

"To-mé's mouth is larger than his ears," said the woman testily. "Po-lone will ride with the chief, or—"

"Or what?" asked To-mé.

"Or she will take down her ho-gan, and ride from the village with her herd."

"Bueno!" exclaimed To-mé. "The heart of the woman is strong."

But Po-lone need not have given herself the trouble to exhibit her annoyance. The chief had no intention whatever to treat her with any marked act of discourtesy. She possessed the largest herds in the clan, and her disaffection would have been a serious blow to his ambition and pride. But he was most anxious now to accomplish a purpose, which he feared might be defeated if Po-lone should accompany him on his journey to the North. He intended, therefore, to withhold the invitation, as long as was possible without giving offense, and thus finally prevent its acceptance.

He had long since determined to purchase the daughter of Po-lone, and he had heretofore attempted to arrange matters in such manner as to leave a quiet field for himself, and thus prepare the way to secure the prize in due time, for a small consideration.

Since the arrival of the runner of the head chief at the lodge of the woman, he had regarded him as a dangerous rival, and had been constantly in fear that the stout-hearted Po-lone, and the impetuous To-mé, would accomplish some unheard of transaction, by which he would lose the girl in the end, and possibly even, the good name of his clan be brought into disrepute in the nation. It was his present purpose, therefore, that To-mé should be gotten quietly away, as quickly as possible, and that the woman and her daughter should remain behind in the village. So far as To-mé was concerned, the chief had found no difficulty in accomplishing his purpose, but it remained yet to be seen how he would succeed in his efforts to control the movements of the woman.

The hour of departure which had been designated by the

chief soon arrived, and one after another,. the principal men
who had been bidden to accompany him to the council, rode
out of the village on the trail to the North. Each one was
followed by two or more squaws, riding astride on rude
sheep-skin saddles, and by one or more peons, driving before them several horses, ladened with robes and with blankets
and food. It was expected that the council would continue
for several days, as had always been the custom on previous occasions, and each warrior, therefore, carried with
him, such supplies as he deemed would be necessary for
himself and his squaws and his peons, during their absence.

The last one of the principal men of the clan had ridden
from the village before the chief made his appearance at
the entrance of his ho-gan. He had dressed himself with
great care, and was resplendent with shining glass beads,
and buttons of silver. His long, black hair had been carefully plaited, and arranged in a mass at the back of his
*head, where it was held in its place by a red ribbon of wool.
From the pendant ends of the ribbon, several immense
feathers were attached, one after the other at short intervals
apart. He wore a new hunting shirt made of deer skin,
and trousers which came to his knees. Tight fitting leggings, extended from his knees to his feet, partially con-
cealing the upper portion of a pair of new moccasins, mag-
nificently embroidered with bright-colored beads, red garnets
and rubies. His broad, leathern girdle was covered with
massive buttons of silver, each as large as the palm of his
hand, and engraved with rude images and characters. An
embroidered band of deer skin hung over his shoulder, to
which a pouch was attached, decorated with the talons of an
eagle, and the claws of a bear, personal trophies of his skill
in the chase. His hunting knife hung conspicuously from his
girdle, and a beaver-skin quiver, containing his bow and

some arrows, was fastened at his back. A multitude of small, flat, silver buttons, covered the outer seams of his trousers and his leggings. Savage ingenuity had exhausted itself, and had left nothing desirable undone.

The chief strutted back and forth in front of his ho-gan, like a very Marquis of Carabas, his soul full of pride and conceit, and his vanity flattered by the admiration of his squaws. At last, mounting his horse which stood ready waiting, he rode directly to the lodge of Po-lone, followed by two runners, a small herd of horses and a few peons and squaws.

"Ho, there!" he cried, reining in his horse at the entrance to the lodge of the woman. "Has Po-lone ridden away with the warriors, and left no one in charge of her ho-gan?"

Even while he spake, Po-lone stood in full view, engaged at some work in her lodge. But he affected not to see her, and addressing himself to the dwarf, who had made his appearance at the entrance, he exclaimed:

"Oh, ho! Mariano judged the woman unwisely. She has ridden to the North, and left Che-no in charge of her ho-gan. That is wise," he said patronizingly. "The woman is wise."

"Nay," replied the woman herself, stepping out of the lodge as she spake. "Po-lone has not ridden to the North."

"How soon will she ride?" he asked quickly.

"Why does the chief ask? Only those ride who are bidden."

"Non-tol-tosh!" cried the chief fiercely, turning as he spake to one of the runners. "Why has not the woman been bidden?"

"The chief spake not her name," replied the runner decidedly.

"Ah!" he said quietly, and turning to the woman he

added in a low, troubled tone, "it is bad. But come now," he added again after a short silence. "Let the woman hasten her work, and make ready to ride. Run, quickly, Che-no," he cried to the dwarf. "Run quick to the herd, and drive in the horses to the lodge."

"Nay," said the woman, "the sun is nearly over the top of the lodge. Let the chief delay no longer for Po-lone."

"The heart of Mariano is sad," he said, slowly, affecting great disappointment, "because Po-lone will not ride. But she is wise," he continued in a more cheerful tone, "and knows best what she should do. She will stay in her ho-gan and take good care of Nah-nee-ta, and when Mariano rides back from the council, he will 'send two of the best horses in his herd to the woman, and Nah-nee-ta shall come and live in the lodge of the chief."

Mariano flattered himself, as he rode slowly away, that his personal appearance had contributed no little to the accomplishment of his purpose, and this pleasant reflection, more than his apparent success, made him supremely happy for the time. As soon as he was well out of sight of the village, he urged his horse forward, and rode rapidly away on the trail of the warriors, closely followed by his runners, while the squaws and the peons came on after with the herd, in the best way they could.

As he disappeared from her view, Po-lone turned quickly about and entered her lodge.

"The young chief has two tongues," she murmured. "He talks to Po-lone with the one that is crooked, and he talks to himself with the other. Po-lone will hearken to the tongue she has heard, and the heart of the chief will then surely be sad. Run quick now Che-no!" she cried to the dwarf. "Run quick to the herd, and drive in the horses. There is no one in the village, so fleet on his feet,

as Cho-no *chiquito*.   Let Po-lone see now, how quick he can
go.''

The dwarf thus encouraged, ran speedily out of the village
on his way to the pastures, and in a short time returned,
driving a number of horses before him.   It required but a
very brief time for Po-lone to complete her preparations,
and an hour had scarcely elapsed before she rode out of the
village accompanied by her daughter, and followed by the
dwarf driving several horses before him, ladened with
blankets and robes, and some parcels of food.

Po-lone at once took the trail of the chief, and rode
steadily on.   It led presently down in a valley which lay
almost concealed at the foot of a range of precipitous mountains on one side, and a broken irregular mountain range,
densely covered with a forest of piñon and pine, on the other.
Occasionally the valley was almost entirely closed by the
encroachment of deep gorges, and immense fields of rock,
pushing down from the broken mountains on the West.   In
such places the trail was forced close up to the perpendicular
wall, sometimes passing over great masses of earth and of
rocks, which at no very remote period, had fallen from the
face of the mountain.   When Po-lone reached these eleva-
tions, she often caught sight of the trail leading away up
the valley for a long distance before her, and several times
she obtained a full view of the lazy warriors, riding leisurely
ahead, closely followed by their squaws and their peons and
herds.

She had often ridden over this trail, and was entirely
familiar with it, throughout its entire extent.   At the
distance of a short day's ride from the village, the broken
mountains suddenly encroached upon the valley and converted it into a cañon that extended for a couple of miles to
the West, and opened at last into a great broad valley be-

yond. Near the middle of the cañon, a great stream of
water burst from the base of the mountain, and, almost
immediately, again disappeared in the rocks. Not far from
this place she knew that the chief would halt for the night.
She moved along leisurely, therefore, not caring to arrive
until the encampment had been formed. At last, just as the
first shades of the evening were beginning to fall, she made
her appearance in the encampment, and rode quietly about,
in such manner as to attract general attention, in search of
a favorable location to make her camp for the night.

At first, the young chief felt greatly annoyed that the
woman had followed his party, and he decided at once to
publicly announce that she had violated the customs of the
nation, in thus following the trail of a chief, without being
formally bidden by the runners. But such a course he soon
reflected, would in all probability cause her to withdraw from
his clan, and might possibly break up the negotiations he
had then in progress for the purchase of her daughter.
Besides, the more he thought upon the subject, the more
convinced he became, that his own course in the matter,
would not meet the approval of the people of his clan. He
decided, therefore, at length, to accept the situation as inevitable, and make the best of it he could. Calling one of
his squaws to him, he sent her directly to say to Po-lone,
that "the heart of the chief was made glad, because the
woman had come."

Immense fires soon lighted up the encampment, and
revealed a weird, busy scene. Several peons and squaws
were engaged here and there, making the necessary preparations to prevent the horses from straying from the camp
during the night. Others were moving rapidly about
gathering wood for the fire, and a few were busily engaged
in cooking the evening meal for their masters and them-

selves. The warriors alone appeared to have nothing to do.
They waited indolently about, squatted down on the ground,
until the squaws could find time from their work to spread
robes on the ground for their use.

At last all the work of the camp was completed. The
necessary fuel had been gathered. All the horses had been
tethered, and the evening meal had been served. The warriors grunted their approval, and soon retired to their robes,
and the squaws wrapping themselves in their blankets, laid
down at the feet of their masters. A deep silence fell on
the encampment. The fires burned low, and fantastic shadows chased one another up and down the great perpendicular wall of the cañon. Finally the fires went out altogether,
and the light faded away in dense, black darkness.

At the first appearance of the light on the following morning, the party was speedily awakened by the watchmen.
Preparations for departure were then hurriedly made, and
when all things were ready the warriors mounted their
horses and rode rapidly away up the cañon, followed by
their dependents and herds.

The distance to the great council chamber from the place
of the encampment was considerably less than a full day's
journey for the party, and when the warriors had gotten
well out of the cañon they slackened their speed and rode
slowly forward, reserving the strength of their horses for a
grand display of their training and speed on arriving at the
mouth of the great council cañon. The chief regarded it as
probable that one or more of the great clans from the North
had already arrived, and he desired to exhibit before them
the marvelous speed of his horses, and the magnificent riding of the warriors of his clan.

Displays of this kind were commonly made by all mounted
parties of warriors at the close of their journeys, unless

some calamity had befallen them while on the way. And it had frequently happened on unimportant occasions that the chief of the clans had purposely delayed their arrival, to secure a large audience to witness the displays they intended. Mariano would now also have gladly delayed for this purpose, but the message of the head chief was urgent, and required immediate compliance. He therefore moved steadily forward until the country about the entrance to the great council cañon was in view. Here the warriors dismounted from their horses to tighten the girths of their saddles, and to make such other preparations as were necessary for the contemplated display. When all these were completed they mounted once more, and rode forward again.

V

The watchman stationed at the entrance to the cañon, a few hundred yards from the great council chamber, shaded his eyes with his hand and looked intently before him, over a broad. level plain, that stretched away to the base of a great mountain range on the east. The runners had already been absent for several days, and the arrival of some of the chiefs of the clans with their principal men, was now constantly expected. A great herd of ponies, belonging to the clan of the head chief, Barbon-ce-to, was quietly grazing not far away in the valley. Beyond, away up to the base of the mountain, not a living thing could be seen. To the north and to the east, as far as the watchman could see, the plain was deserted. The savage turned his head wearily, and gazed for a moment to the south. Minute, black objects, scarcely discernable, even to the practiced eye of the watchman, were moving about near the horizon, quivering and trembling like uneasy spirits in the burdened air.

"Muchacho! Muchacho!" cried the savage at length, to a little naked urchin who stood near him. "Run quick to the chief, and say that the watchman sees horsemen, far away in the south."

In the meantime the black objects gradually came nearer, assuming mere forms as they came. They grew tall and slender, and moved up and down with uncertain and fantastic motion. At length they began to acquire more definite shape, and the exaggerated outlines of horses and men could be discerned. These in their turn, gradually gave way to more natural forms, and eventually a great cavalcade of mounted savages suddenly burst out of the *mirage* and galloped in full view towards the entrance of the cañon.

Upon being informed of the approach of the horsemen, the head chief at once hastened to the entrance of the cañon and took a conspicuous position on a great flat rock by the side of the watchman, to honor their arrival by his presence. In the meantime a large number of the people of his clan hurried to the tops of the great rocks that lay about the north of the cañon, to witness the anticipated display of the clan from the South.

But the people were doomed to disappointment. Mariano had observed as he approached, that not one of the chiefs of all the clans of the nation, had yet arrived at the cañon. He decided, therefore, that he would make no display, and hastened forward at once to complete the brief ceremony, which custom was required from representative of a clan, on his arrival in the presence of the head chief of the nation. Galloping rapidly forward at the head of his warriors, he wheeled them quickly into line, and brought them to a halt in front of the cañon. When this movement was completed he rode forward a short distance alone, and then dismounted before the head chief, as an expression of respect and submission. So soon as this formal act had been acknowledged, he again mounted his horse and returned to his warriors. Wheeling them about he rode rapidly away in the direction from which he had come.

When he had ridden a fair hundred yards from the entrance of the cañon, he drew a barbed arrow from his quiver, and sent it from his bow to a great height in the air. It fell to the earth and imbedded itself in the ground, almost to the feather. Riding to the spot he hastily dismounted, and taking his buckskin lariat from his saddle, he sent it spinning in a coil about the arrow. He had thus chosen his camping ground for himself and his clan, and the arrow from his quiver was suffered to remain where it fell, as a silent witness of his right to the place, which no one would dare to dispute.

The squaws and the peons soon arrived with the herds, and the encampment was speedily formed.

As soon as it became apparent that the clan of Mariano would not make a display, the head chief retired into the cañon by the way he had come, and the people rapidly dispersed from the rocks. They had scarcely all found their way down, when the watchman gave notice that a great party of horsemen was approaching from the north. The rocks about the mouth of the cañon were almost immediately covered again with the people. One of the great clans from the north was approaching, and to sustain its reputation, a grand display of the horsemanship of its warriors would doubtless be made. The disappointment which the people had experienced on the arrival of the clan from the south, had apparently increased their eagerness to witness a display, and they crowded and jostled each other in their efforts to obtain desirable places on the rocks.

The young chief had established his camp directly south of the entrance to the cañon, and near the foot of the mountain through which it passed. The base of the mountain near his encampment was fringed with great rocks which had been detached from its side and had fallen below.

Mariano and his warriors hastened to these rocks, and selecting those most accessible, clambered to their summits. The great plain lay spread out before them, bathed in a flood of soft sunlight, that fell gently upon it through the dense, hazy air.

The head chief again made his appearance at the entrance to the cañon, and took his formal place by the side of the watchman. The busy voices of the women and the peons rose in a volume at times, like an impatient murmur, and lingered in the caverns among the great rocks. The warriors stood apart from each other wrapped in their blankets, silent and motionless as statues.

As the horsemen approached nearer, the people on the rocks recognized the chief riding in advance.

"It is the clan of the war chief," they cried one to another, "and Manu-le-to himself rides before it."

This clan was the largest in the nation, and its warriors bore the reputation of being most accomplished as horsemen. Its chief was a warrior of renown who for a long time had held the office of war-chief of the nation, a position scarcely less important than that held by the head chief himself.

To the war-chief was invariably intrusted the supreme control of all the chiefs of the clans, and their warriors under them, when their services were required on the warpath. He was, in short, the commander-in-chief of all the forces of the nation when called out by the head chief or the council.

The authority of the two chiefs was clearly defined by the condition of public affairs. The one was supreme when the nation was at peace, the other when the nation was at war.

Manu-le-to rode in front of his warriors, galloping quietly along near the base of the mountain towards the entrance to the cañon. At a signal, his followers formed suddenly in line, and swept past the spectators in perfect order, like a troop of trained cavalry. When they had gone fairly past they wheeled quickly about, and urging their horses to greater speed than before, once more swept over the ground. When they arrived at a point directly in front of the head chief, they suddenly wheeled to the left and instantly came to a halt facing the cañon.

Manu-le-to then dismounted in token of submission to the

authority of the head chief of the nation, and advanced a
few paces towards him.   The head chief bowed in response,
and Manu-le-to turning immediately to his horse, mounted
quickly again, and rode back to his warriors.   As he
reached them, those on the right of the center of the line
moved forward a short distance, and turning their horses
rode back to their places, leaving an unoccupied space of
several feet between the platoons.   Those on the left of the
line still faced to the west, while those on the right now
faced to the east.

 At a signal, the platoons began to move in a circle like
the arms of a great wheel revolving about on its axis.   At
first they moved slowly, but their speed gradually increased
until the two arms at last revolved with such wonderful
rapidity that their identity was almost lost to the view of
the people.   A great cloud of dust arose quickly about them
and finally concealed them entirely from view.   In an instant, thereafter, the platoons reappeared, one flying to the
north and the other to the south.   The great cloud of dust
ascended in the air, and continued the motion it had received from the circling platoons.   At last it resolved itself
into a whirlwind and swept with tremendous violence
across the great plain to the east.

The platoons at length wheeled once more about, and
came sweeping back in the same order as before.   They
passed by the chief at almost the same instant, the right
horseman of one of the platoons and the left horseman of
the other, barely missing him as they passed.   Arriving at
the extremities of the course, the platoons once more
wheeled about, and came flying back towards each other
again.   The chief speedily moved from between them and
gave a signal with his hand.   Instantly each warrior threw
himself on the side of his horse out of view of the people.

The horses, now apparently riderless, continued their flight without in the least abating their wonderful speed. When the platoons arrived near to each other, the riders suddenly made their appearance on the backs of their horses. Many of them rose to their knees, some sprang to their feet, all of them drew their tomahawks or their knives, and, with loud shouts and yells, they rode pell-mell against one another, brandishing their weapons the meanwhile, and striking to the right and to the left in the most extravagant and desperate manner. An instant thereafter the platoons passed through each other, as neatly and completely as ones fingers are passed when the hands are clasped together.

Once more the platoons reached the ends of the course, and again wheeling about, came rushing at each other with tremendous force. Again the battle charge was repeated, and again the platoons passed through each other, with amazing skill and precision. Then they wheeled on the same ground as before, and almost instantly came to a halt.

An apparently riderless horse now sprang immediately from one of the platoons, and ran at great speed along the course. When he reached a point opposite the cañon, a warrior raised himself from his concealment on the side of the animal, and springing to his feet, discharged a number of harmless reed arrows, in rapid succession at the people. Finally, he sent one directly before him, and seizing the mane of his horse, he sprang nimbly to the ground, as he dashed past the spot when it lay, and seized it with his hand. In an instant he sprang again on the back of his horse and waved the arrow triumphantly over his head. Turning his horse quickly about, he rode back to his platoon, and was received by his comrades with shouts of applause.

The rival platoon answered these shouts with yells of de-

fiance, and at once sent a champion out on the course to
make a still more marvelous display. He rode forward at a
tremendous pace, stretched out at full length upon the back
of his horse, his feet locked together on the animal's breast.
Suddenly he threw himself forward and revolved several
times in rapid succession about the animals neck. Instantly
a great shout arose from his comrades, at both ends of the
course, and the excited people joined with them, and prolonged the applause until the champion returned to his
place.

Another rider now galloped out from the other platoon.
When he arrived near the center of the course, he sprang
suddenly to the ground, and permitted his horse to escape.
As the animal galloped away he called it by name, and bade
it return. The obedient creature, at once turned and galloped towards him. As it came near, the warrior ran forward to meet it, and sprang upon its back without arresting
its speed.

Again a champion appeared from the rival platoon, galloping quietly along the course. When he arrived nearly
opposite the entrance to the cañon, he sprang from his horse,
and fell to the ground. The animal stopped instantly, and
walked slowly about the prostrate form of his master. At
last the horse touched him with its nose, and pushed him
with some force. His master then arose to his feet, and
springing upon the animal's back, returned to his place.

Two warriors now rode from each of the platoons, and
hastened to meet on the course. As they came near to each
other, they threw themselves on the sides of their horses,
and began circling around one another, and discharging reed
arrows, as though actually engaged in a battle. At last,
one of the warriors feigned he was wounded, and fell from
his horse to the ground. The animal immediately galloped

away, but at the call of his master returned to him again.
The warrior then feigned that he was unable to remount, and
after several attempts, lay down on the ground. His companion hastened to his assistance, and seizing him by his
strong leathern girdle raised him up before him on his
horse. Then instantly detaching his lariat from his saddle,
he cast the loop dextrously over the head of the horse of his
wounded companion, and at once galloped away at full
speed, hotly pursued for a while, by the warriors who
feigned the part of his enemies.

Manu-le-to now signaled his warriors to advance, and
having formed them again into line, rode on before them
until he arrived near the ground occupied by the clan of the
young chief. Then seizing an arrow from his quiver he sent
it from his bow to a great height in the air. When it fell
to the ground he rode hastily to the spot, and dismounting
from his horse, coiled his lariat about it. His squaws and
his peons, who had been waiting near by, now rode forward
with the herds, and the encampment of the war chief was
speedily formed.

Night soon came on, and little fires sprang up here and
there throughout the encampment. The warriors gathered
in groups, and sat smoking, and gravely talking upon subjects of common interest to all. The squaws also gathered
in groups by themselves, and talked glibly to one another
about the blankets they had made since the last council met,
and praised the horses in the herds of their masters, and
retailed the gossip of their village.

Po-lone could not mingle with the women. Neither
could she sit in the groups with the men. The women
were servants, and the men were all warriors. She was
simply a person holding a position above the common lot of
her sex, by virtue of her possessions. She sat by her fire

quietly conversing with her daughter, and listening now and then to the busy voices of the women about her.

Nah-nee-ta had never before witnessed such wonderful displays as she had witnessed that day, and for a time, she could think of nothing but the trained, flying horses, and the marvelous deeds of their riders. Po-lone finally grew weary with answering her questions, and the girl longed for some one with whom she could talk. If To-mé would only come, he could tell her the names of the riders, and how they had learned to accomplish such wonderful things.

But where was To-mé! He had left the encampment in the cañon, she had heard, at some time during the night, but no one could tell her where he had gone. She had looked for him in every direction all the day long. She grew weary, at last, with her thoughts, and sinking down on her robe, fell fast asleep.

Po-lone at once rose to her feet, and wrapping her blanket about her, stole quietly away. Approaching the nearest group of the warriors, she stopped at a short distance from it, and concealed by the darkness, gazed at the warriors intently.

"He is not among them," she said at length, to herself, and passed on to continue her search.

Po-lone was once more sorely perplexed. To-mé had not given so hearty an acquiescence to the proposal she had made, as she could have desired, and she feared that the young man had taken himself away to avoid further committal. That he had absented himself now, at so important a time, served further to strengthen her fears. It was barely possible, however, that he had gone on some duty, and had been unexpectedly delayed. She would have given the best horse in the herd for any reasonable assurance that her fears had been needlessly awakened.

She moved noiselessly about from one group to another, listening to the voices of the warriors as they conversed among themselves, not caring to hear what was said, but listening only for the voice of To-mé. She listened in vain. To-mé was not among them, and she returned at length to her fire, more perplexed, if it were possible, than ever.

She had scarcely again taken her seat when she was startled by the sudden appearance of a strange-looking man standing near her, and gazing intently in her face. She had heard no approaching footsteps to warn her of the coming of the mysterious stranger, and her mind was at once filled with the most serious apprehensions. She was only able to attribute his noiseless approach to the exercise of some supernatural power, and she returned his fixed gaze with undisguised astonishment and awe.

At length she glanced furtively about her, with the hope that some one might be near, upon whom she could depend for assistance. A few squaws sat chattering together in a group about a little fire not very far from her, but she reflected at once, that her first cry of alarm would frighten them away. Turning again to the stranger, she looked once more in his face. He still stood in the place where he had made his appearance, apparently waiting until she should recover her composure. His kindly face served in some manner to reassure her, and she gradually gathered courage to observe him more closely.

He was richly but peculiarly dressed. His hunting shirt and his leggins were colored intensely black, and were ornamented extravagantly with small silver buttons. A crescent-shaped amulet, from which curious charms hung, was clasped on his neck by a band, made from the bright spotted skin of a snake.

"Whom does Po-lone seek among the warriors?" he demanded at length, in a tone of authority.

"Po-lone seeks no one," she replied tremulously, "and knows not who asks her the question."

"The woman hears the words of Me-su-la, the great medicine man of the clan of the head chief, Barbon-ce-to," said the stranger, with great deliberation.

"The feet of the medicine man must be weary," said Po-lone, hastening to spread a robe on the ground for his use.

"Yea, the feet of the old are always weary," he said; and throwing his blanket aside, he seated himself on the robe.

"How came Me-su-la so noiselessly to the fire?" she asked, timorously. "Did he drop from the clouds, or did he come up from the caverns in the earth?"

"Me-su-la followed the woman to her fire, but her ears were both closed to the noise of his feet."

The old man then bowed his head on his breast and covered his face with his hands, and for some time remained silent. In the meanwhile, the woman sat quietly in her place, watching the fire as it burned, and patiently waiting for the medicine man to make known the object of his visit. At last he raised up his head, and looking at her intently, said sternly:

"The woman is in trouble."

"Let Me-su-la speak on," she replied.

"Let Po-lone answer, if she will, or Me-su-la will find no more words in his mouth."

"Po-lone is in trouble," she said hesitatingly.

"Because she could not hear the voice of the runner, To-mé?"

"Yea, the words of the medicine man are all true. He has heard the Great Spirit speak, and knows many things."

"The woman is wise," he said quietly. "She must have patience, and wait. The light of the sun will scarcely drive the shadows from the valleys again, before the runner will return. The daughter of the woman will be happy in the lodge of To-mé."

"Nay!" she cried hurriedly, "he desires not—"

"Desires not the maiden!" interrupted Me-su-la in a tone of astonishment. "Po-lone has not looked well in his face, nor hearkened aright to his words. Listen now to the words of the medicine man. To-mé will take the girl to his lodge. Whoever says nay, and stands in the way, will offend the Great Spirit. Let the woman cease now to trouble herself. Me-su-la has spoken."

Rising slowly to his feet he drew his blanket about him, and walked deliberately away, without speaking again. Po-lone watched his retreating form until it was lost in the darkness, and then springing to her feet she walked impatiently back and forth in front of her fire.

"Yea," she murmured, at length, to herself, "the medicine man has spoken to Po-lone, and she has heard all his words. But the end is not yet. Me-su-la must talk once again with the Great Spirit. He shall choose a horse from the herd of the woman, and then he may hear words to gladden her heart."

Po-lone was evidently well pleased with the course she had determined to pursue, and she nodded her head confidently, as though she already foresaw its eventual success. She came back directly and resumed her seat at the fire, as quietly and unconcernedly as though nothing whatever had even occurred to disturb her composure.

She had scarcely again seated herself, when the camp was suddenly startled by a cry from the watchman. The warriors sprang instantly to their feet, and hastened to the mouth of the cañon, to learn the cause of the alarm. They found Barbon-ce-to already at his post on the rocks, await-

ing their arrival. Addressieg himself to the war chief
Manu-le-to, he informed him that one of his runners had
discovered a number of strange warriors riding rapidly
down from the north towards the encampments. No time
must be lost, for the strangers were not far away. If they
were enemies, they must not be permitted to reach the encampments, and if they should prove to be friends, it would
be desirable to know what had prompted their journey in
the country of the nation at such an unusual hour.

The warriors dispersed instantly, and ran speedily to their
several encampments. At the first note of alarm, the squaws
had saddled the fleetest horses in the herds and now held
them in readiness for the use of their masters. The warriors hastily mounted and galloped away, and soon disappeared in the darkness.

To the north of the country occupied by the Nation,
lived a great and warlike tribe of nomads, known as the
Utes. The Navajos had been at peace with this tribe for
many long years, but there now existed some cause for complaint. The Utes had encroached upon the pasture grounds
of the nation, and some acts of violence had already been
committed. It was possible, therefore, that the strangers
might be a strong party of Utes, rough riding through the
country, taking advantage of the temporary absence of the
chiefs and the principal men of the clans, to capture their
horses and burn their ho-gans.

The two chiefs rode forward together, closely followed by
their warriors. Not a word had been uttered since they had
ridden from the encampments, and the great silence about
them was unbroken, save by the pattering feet of their
horses as they galloped over the plain. At length the
chiefs brought their horses to a walk and Manu-le-to, addressing his companion, said briefly ;

"Let my brother move slowly forward along the base of the mountain. Manu-le-to will ride out on the plain. If enemies are found, let few arrows fly. The knife of a warrior is his best friend in the dark."

Mariano at once moved away in the direction of the mountain, closely followed by his warriors.

The two parties now acting independently drew rapidly apart, and were soon out of sight of each other. They had gone on for some time eagerly watching and listening, when suddenly a great shout arose at a point not far in advance of the party of the chief Manu-le-to. No response was returned, and the party rode steadily forward. Again the cry came, more distinct than before, and mingled with it could be heard the voices of people engaged in conversation. Little fires soon appeared, and as the warriors approached, they could distinctly observe a number of squaws running hither and thither engaged in the usual labor of the camp. This was clearly no party with warlike intentions, but Manu-le-to's long experience as a warrior had taught him that he might often expect danger, where it seemed least likely to be found. The party before him was certainly not feared, but it was yet to be determined whether it was not being used to cover the movements of an accompanying expedition.

Leaving a single warrior behind him, with directions to advance into the camp of the strangers when he should hear the repeated cry of a coyote from the north, he moved cautiously forward with the others. Keeping the fires in view, he circled around the encampment to the north, without discovering any evidence of an outlying party of warriors. At last he halted his command, and caused one of his warriors to imitate the cry of a coyote. The wailing cry had scarcely died away in the air before it was answered by a similar cry from the south. Again the warrior at the side of the chief repeated the plaintive cry, and again it was answered from the south. Presently a loud shout was heard not far from the camp, answered almost immediately by another. Then other shouts followed, and again all was silent.

At last, after considerable time had elapsed, a single horseman galloped out from the camp and rode to the north. As he approached he was recognized as the warrior who had been left behind by the chief, and his comrades at once crowded eagerly about him to learn what had occurred. Addressing himself to Manu-le-to, he briefly informed him that the strangers were friendly Utes accompanied by their squaws, going down to the encampments near the great council chamber, with running horses and robes. They had been detained by an accident to one of their people some time during the day, and had therefore been unable to reach a suitable place for their camp at an earlier hour. Their leader had then caused frequent shouts to be made in order that their peaceable character might not be mistaken, should their presence be discovered.

The war chief was well satisfied, from the account of the warrior, that there was no further cause to apprehend any danger, but he deemed it yet due to his great reputation as a vigilant leader that he should obtain further evidence that the strangers had not misrepresented themselves.

Detaching a runner at once from his party, he sent him with orders to find the young chief, and direct him to deploy his command, and cause his warriors to ride back and forth across the great plain for a considerable distance to the east. In the meantime he remained where he was to watch the camp of the Utes.

After the lapse of some time the young chief came in

with his warriors, He had thoroughly searched over the
plain, for a long distance to the east, and found it entirely
deserted.

There was now nothing more to be done. Every effort
to discover an inimical intent on the part of the Utes
had utterly failed.

Their peaceable intentions were established beyond
question.

"My brother," said Manu-le-to, addressing the young
chief, "the enemies of the nation are hard always to find.
Let the warriors return to the encampments."

The whole party instantly set out without further command and galloped furiously back to the south. As it approached the encampments the watchman stationed at the
entrance of the cañon again gave the alarm, and the few
warriors who had remained for the protection of the camp
gathered hurriedly together. The head chief himself hastened to join them to encourage them by his presence. But
all apprehensions were speedily removed by the well-known
shouts of the warriors, announcing their return. Almost
immediately thereafter, they came suddenly in view, galloping madly towards the mouth of the cañon, uttering
fierce yells and brandishing their weapons as they came.
Then, at a word from the chief, they dispersed quickly to
their several encampments, and hastily dismounting, delivered their horses into the care of the,rsquaws.

VI.

To-mé had at first, rather hastily determined to accept the woman's offer and abandon the idea of purchasing her daughter. The difficulties which presented themselves in the way of accomplishing what he desired, appeared to him at the time, to be utterly insurmountable, and he reasoned, therefore, that it was best to accept the offer which the woman had made, and sacrifice his new-formed inclinations to his permanent advantage.

But when he awoke on the following morning and recalled what he had done, he regretted his haste, and immediately began to discuss in his mind the feasibility of one plan and another, by which he might be able to retain the confidence of the woman and hold the refusal of her offer, to be finally accepted if his future negotiations for the daughter should fail.

He thought the subject all over, without being able to arrive at a different conclusion. This was doubtless fortunate for To-mé, and saved him the mortification of a possible failure thereafter.

It is certainly an abnormal condition of the mind that actuates an individual, after laborious thoughts have been given, to undertake the performance of some secret scheme, which by its very nature makes his object apparent to others. So, for a notable example, Trochu's great plan for the defence of Paris against the Prussians, conceived with much labor, and undertaken with secrecy almost dramatic, was apparent to the enemy from the first.

To-mé was several times on the eve of carrying out what appeared to be a well digested plan, but fortunately hesitated as often, and eventually left the matter in abeyance until he could think more of it.

At last, at the very moment when the woman and her daughter made their appearance in the encampment of the chief, he determined upon a course that he then thought of for the first time. He would hasten to his powerful friend, the great medicine man, Me-su-la, and lay the matter before him, and request his advice and assistance.

Early on the following morning before, any of the people were awake, he mounted his horse and rode away up the cañon. Leaving the main traveled trail, he turned his horse into a path that gradually ascended along the face of the precipitous mountain on his right. Horsemen seldom attempted to ascend by this trail, and it was almost entirely abandoned to the sheep and the goats. He could have gone farther on and found a safe trail, but he was now in great haste, and his impatient spirit could bear no delay. Dismounting at once he began the ascent, leading the horse on behind him.

For the entire distance, from the base of the mountain to its summit, the path followed a narrow shelf on the face of the wall, scarcely wide enough often to permit the passage of his horse. Here and there it was crossed by deep furrows, worn by great torrents of water that had fallen at times from the summit of the mountain, and far up near the top it was crossed by a chasm that seemed almost impossible to pass.

To-mé slowly climbed up the trail, and at last reached tl edge of the chasm. He stood for a moment undecided, and then sprang nimbly across and attempted to lead his horse after. But the animal stubbornly refused to follow. Time and again he led him up to the deep, silent chasm, but as frequently the terrified animal drew suddenly back and attempted to escape by the way he had come. To-mé at last got behind him, and forced him forward by main strength to the brink. With a great cry of terror the affrighted animal sprang over the chasm and hastened on up the narrow trail. The summit was then speedily reached, and To-mé, hastily mounting, rode quickly away across the broad, level *mesa*, that crowned the top of the mountain.

The sun was near the meridian when the runner came in sight of a little valley, many weary miles distant from the encampment he had left in the morning. He rode slowly forward and entered the valley, looking to the right and the left in the chaparral of stunted growths of piñon and pines, which here and there skirted its sides, for some indication of the object of his search. At length he observed numerous trails made by horses and sheep, diverging from one of the groves down into the valley. Guided by these certain indications of the proximity of a village, he rode towards the grove from which the trails came. As he approached nearer he heard the voices of people, and at last came directly upon the hogan of Me-su-la, the great medicine man of the clan of the head chief Barbon-ce-to, standing in the center of the grove, and almost concealed by the thick undergrowth about it. Me-su-la himself stood at the door of his ho-gan, and as To-mé came near, called him by name, and bade him welcome. The weary horse of· the runner was speedily transferred to the care of a squaw, and sent to the best pasture grounds in the valley, and a robe was spread on the floor of the lodge for the warrior, upon which he might rest until some food could be prepared.

To-mé was highly pleased with the kind reception he had met, and he accepted it as a certain indication that he would be able to obtain the good services of his host, in his professional capacity as a medicine maker. This was indeed very fortunate, and To-mé had good reason to be pleased. There were so many contingencies and essential conditions in the medicine man's calendar, so many uncontrollable things seldom in harmony that must work together to insure a successful result, that long periods often intervened, during which he was incapable of offering his services to his people. The moon and certain stars had to be carefully consulted; the wanderings of the sheep, and the direction of flights of certain rare birds, had also to be watched; and, last of all, but by no means the least, it was necessary that a vision by night should appear to some one in the village. A dream of some kind or other, merely to give indication to the medicine man that the Great Unknown Cause had come within his reach. When all of these things were propitious, his face wore a smile, and he was happy and kind. His visitors needed not to be told that the signs were all good, and that medicine could be made, or that they were bad and nothing could be done. The appearance of the medicine man's face told the whole story, and time after time when the necessary conditions were unfavorable, his anxious visitors went silently away so soon as they caught sight of his gloomy countenance.

Medicine making was deemed a most important observance, and was usually undertaken to secure the intervention of supernatural power, for good or for evil. It had no special reference to pharmacy alone, but included with it invocations and conjurings, the preparation of charms, and other mysterious processes, employed to influence a desired result.

Warriors made medicine to induce the Great Spirit to make them strong when in battle, and successful in destroying their enemies. They made medicine to enable them to determine the result of some expedition they intended, or to insure its success. The warriors, however, were not able to make medicine, that could be depended upon always as infallible. This power could only be exercised in its perfec-

tion by the professional medicine man of the Nation, who
held the great secrets of the necessary ceremonials and conditions, which alone could be relied upon to influence supernatural intervention. They were, in short, the chief priests
of the nation, and their curative preparations, and their
charms, and their words of advice and instruction, were regarded as due to direct revelations from the Great Spirit
himself.

To-mé had often made medicine on ordinary occasions,
but the matter now involved he regarded as of unusual importance. His imperfect knowledge of the art might possibly lead him astray, and all his efforts prove utterly useless.
He had come, therefore, to lay the whole subject before the
greatest sorcerer in the nation, and to ask his kindly services in his behalf.

When he had eaten the food that had been set before him,
and he had smoked a friendly pipe with his host, he proceeded to make known the object of his visit. Beginning
with his arrival at the village of the young chief, he related
the whole story of his adventures, up to the time of his arrival at the ho-gan of Me-su-la. In the sententious language
of his people, he told of the girl's beauty and his great desire to carry her to his cheerless ho-gan ; of the proposition
of the woman and his hasty acceptance ; and how, now, he depended at last upon the words and the counsel of the great
medicine man, to guide his course in the future.

Me-su-la listened in silence until To-mé had concluded,
and then addressing himself to his visitor, said quietly:

"To-mé should be wise."

"And what should To-mé do to be wise?" he asked, somewhat impatiently.

"It would be wise for a warrior to turn his herd into one
that is larger," replied Me-su-la with provoking deliberation.

"Then To-mé does not wish to be wise," he said petu-lently. And then after a short pause he added, "unless there is no other way."

"Bah!" said the old man sharply. "To-mé is a fool. What does he want in the ho-gan of Me-su-la? Let him speak quickly."

"To-mé desires the great medicine man to make medi-cine for him, and then speak the words that the great spirit has put in his mouth, not alone to To-mé but also to the woman. To-mé will hearken to the words and obey them every one, whatever they may be, and Me-su-la shall choose the best horse in To-mé's herd for his own."

"Let To-mé hearken to the words of Me-su-la," urged the old man. "Let him accept the good offer that the woman has made, and cease to think more of the girl."

"To-mé can never be happy until he has taken the girl home to his lodge," he said dejectedly.

"Bah!" said the old man, "To-mé should cease to be a warrior. His heart has grown soft. Bah!" he repeated in-dignantly, "To-mé's eyes have grown weak. He cannot see now as far as he can shoot."

To-mé bowed down his head, but made no reply.

"Bah!" continued the old man. "It is idle for a war-rior to talk of being happy, before the spirit land has been reached. Let To-mé hearken well to the words of Me-su-la. The beautiful Nah-nee-ta is a Mexican."

"It is possible," said To-mé quietly. "How does Me-su-la know that the girl is a Mexican?"

"Does To-mé ask the medicine man how he knows what has happened in the past? Let him ask rather, how he knows what will happen in the future."

"Let Me-su-la speak on."

"Yea, Me-su-la will speak once again. To-mé refuses to be wise. He refuses to hearken to the counsel of his friend.

He comes to the ho-gan of the medicine man, and demands that medicine shall be made, and the great spirit asked to put pleasant words into the mouth of Me-su-la.''

The old man ceased to speak, and for a time gazed vacantly before him. At length he continued.

''It is done, even as To-mé demanded, and the pleasant words which he desired have been spoken. The woman has heard them, and has hastened to obey. To-mé's heart has been filled with great joy, and he has taken the maiden to his lodge. One of his horses has gone to the herd of the medicine man, and now he sends three others to the herd of the woman. To-mé has but one left. But why should he care? His heart is now happy, and his lodge is made bright by the smiles of the maiden.

''One moon passes away, and then another one passes, and at last the snow falls again upon the mountains and whitens their tops. A warrior comes riding in great haste to the lodge and cries, 'Me-ra,' my brother, the war chief goes soon to the country of the Apaches, and he desires that To-mé shall make ready to ride. Each warrior must take three horses in his herd. Hasten my brother to the gathering at the great council chamber.'' Can To-mé make ready to ride? Nay, he has but one horse, and he says in his sorrow, 'had To-mé been wise he might go as a chief.'

''Again a warrior comes riding to the lodge, and as he draws near he cries; 'Hasten, my brother, to join the chief of the clan, to hunt the antelope in the valleys below.' To-mé's heart bounds with joy, and he hastens to seize his bow and his quiver. But he stops quickly as he recalls his impoverished condition. No hunter could go on such a chase, with only one horse. He hides his face in his hands, and says to himself, 'if To-mé had been wise, he might ride with the hunters on the fleetest horses in the clan.'

"At length the beautiful Nah-nee-ta grows weary in her lodge, and asks to be taken for a time, to the ho-gan of her mother. How shall she go? To-mé has but one horse. Shall a squaw ride on a horse with a warrior? Nay, that is impossible, and the squaw soon grows sad, and To-mé is unhappy in his lodge.

"But evils come never alone. At last the horse sickens and dies, and To-mé wanders about like a beggar, on foot, the poorest warrior in the tribe. Bah! there he goes," cried the old man excitedly, shading his eyes with his hand as he spake, and looking intently before him. "Bah! there he goes, a poor wretch, on foot and alone. He refused to be wise. Let him suffer.

"Nay, nay," he cried suddenly. "Me-su-la sees him not. It was all a bad dream. To-mé has been wise. He has accepted the good offer which the woman has made. He has turned his horses into the herd of Po-lone, and lives in the ho-gan with the woman. To-mé is now happy indeed, and his heart has grown light."

"Bah!" said To-mé. "Can a warrior be happy, in the ho-gan of the mother of a Mexican?"

"Bah!" ejaculated the old man. "To-mé is a fool."

"Can a warrior be happy before the spirit land has been reached?" asked To-mé.

"Bah!" repeated the old man. "To-mé has but the half of a head."

"The medicine man can talk as he pleases. His words are all hot, but they burn not in the ears of To-mé."

"A warrior cannot be truly happy," said the medicine man kindly, as though he desired to atone for the harsh words he had used, "until his spirit has reached the eternal country of the dead. He may be contented for a day, or even for a moon, but, sooner or later, the evil spirit will enter his ho_

gan and pierce him with arrows unseen, to poison his heart
and wound his flesh with disease."

"The evil spirit would flee from the presence of the beautiful Nah-nee-ta," said To-mé.

"Bah!" replied the old man. "What is a squaw, that
To-mé should speak thus of the girl? The great spirit made
the squaws to be servants for his people. They die, and
their spirits go into the fish, that live in the waters. Nah-
nee-ta may seem to please To-mé for a day, or even for a
moon, and drive the shadows from his lodge, but what more
can she do? In the end, she will go to her place in the
waters, and To-mé will travel alone on his journey to the
country of the dead."

"The journey is a long one," said To-mé, musingly.
"And when a warrior is dead, his friends burn his body,
that his spirit may not be wearied with a useless burden on
the way."

"Yea, yea," said the old man, bowing his head as he
spoke. "That his body may not be a useless burden on the
way."

"And horses are killed and their bodies are burned, that
the spirit of the dead warrior may ride upon the spirits of
the dead horses on his journey."

"Yes," said the old man, "and To-mé should be wise or
he may not leave a horse to be killed when he dies."

"And his bow and his quiver full of arrows are burned
also, that he may use them on the way."

"Yes."

"And the journey is a long one," he repeated, "and
many moons pass away before the end has been reached."

"Yes."

"It were best then," said To-mé, "that the warrior
should take a squaw with him to serve him on the way."

"Would To-mé have a squaw killed like a horse?"

"Nay," said To-mé, "but the spirit of the one who dies first might hide in the shadows of the cañon, or in the corners in the mountains and wait for the other."

"Nay," said the old man. "The Great Spirit has not put such words in the mouth of To-mé. The spirits of the horses cease to exist when the warrior reaches the end of his journey. But the spirit of a squaw cannot cease to exist, neither can it go from the earth. In the country of the dead, the most beautiful squaws wait even now, in ho-gans of sweet smelling cedar, for the coming of their masters from the land of the mortals.

"Nay, nay, the squaws of the earth are for this life alone. Not even the beautiful Nah-nee-ta can go with To-mé on his journey to the country of the dead. Many dangers and trials are met on the way, and the spirits of many brave warriors grow weary and faint before the end has been reached, and are forever destroyed. A squaw cannot go on the war path because her heart is not strong. How then can her spirit go on the journey to the country of the dead? Has To-mé wise words in his mouth to reply?"

"Nay, To-mé has no words in his mouth to reply, but his ears are both open to hearken to the words of the Medicine Man. Will Me-su-la speak on?"

"Of what does the warrior wish Me-su-la to speak!"

"Of the long journey and the dangers on the way. Of the country of the dead, and the pleasures which await the warriors who reach it."

"Brave To-mé has found his head once again," cried the old man joyfully, "and his words are all wise. Me-su-la will speak and the warrior shall hearken, that his heart may grow strong."

To-mé eagerly leaned forward towards him, to catch every word he would utter, but the Medicine Man suddenly dropped his head on his breast, and for a long time remained silent. After several minutes had elapsed, To-mé began really to fear that the old man had forgotten his presence or had fallen asleep. But he knew well the custom of the Medicine Man and waited on patiently yet for awhile, hoping that the silence would soon be broken. At last the old man raised up his head, and looking intently at To-mé, began to speak in a tone scarcely audible.

"When a warrior is dead," he said slowly, "and his body been burned, his spirit takes the form in which it lived on the earth, and starts at once for the country of the dead. His spirit can never more suffer from hunger or from thirst, from heat or from cold, or from the recollections of the miseries of the life that has closed. In all other things there has been little change, except that his powers which remain have grown very strong. His spirit feels pain and enjoys pleasure more intensely than ever before. The slightest noise can be heard and the most distant objects can be seen.

"His spirit starts on its journey very happy and free—as light as the sun and as pure as the air in the mountains—rid of the burden of a useless body, and of all care to provide means to prolong its existence, rid of greasy hunting shirts and of dirty leggins, and rid—best of all—rid of squaws with long tongues, and of smoking ho-gans. His spirit has grown strong as the claws of a grizzly monster in the mountain, and feet as the feet of the antelope in the valley. He travels on his journey as he pleases, and grows never weary. There are no shadows to fall across the trail that he follows, for he sees alike well in the dark and in the light. There are no evil spirits now to torment him, and he sleeps not for he never needs rest.

"At last, after many, many moons have passed away, his spirit enters into the land of the Chiquitos, the dreaded dwarfs who have ever been on the war path against the spirits of mortals which have entered their country. His quick ear at once catches the sound of many alarms, and he knows that the time has now come for his trial.

"If his spirit can be driven back from where it has come, or it fails in the courage or the skill of the warrior, it forever ceases to exist. But if it proves to be brave and to be skillful, and meets the dangers in the way without fear, it overcomes all its enemies and at last reaches the end of the long journey in triumph. Let To-mè keep his heart strong, that he may be prepared for the last trial through which he must pass.

"The Chiquitos are dwarfs, but they must not be despised. They are active and brave on the war path and full of strange devices to deceive the spirit of the warrior whose heart is not strong. They are not spirits for they have a body of flesh with all of its burdens; neither are they mortals, for they cannot be found by a living warrior. They vanish into the air like the snake of the lodge fin when they are wounded, and then forever disappear.

"It matters not what existence they have, they are the last deadly enemies of the warriors, hiding on the border of the country of the dead, to destroy their spirits as they pass. Let the smoke of their vile bodies mark the trail of the spirit at every step of its journey through their evil land.

The bodies of the Chiquitos are covered with immense ears, that extend from the top of their hairless heads to their feet, and serve to protect them from the heat and the cold. When they desire rest or concealment, they lie down upon one of their ears, and close the other upon it.

"The spirit of the warrior, as it passes through their country, comes often upon them, in hiding or asleep. If the spirit kicks them with its foot, or strikes them with its bow, they thrust at it spitefully, with lances made from thorns of the cactus, and hasten away howling like wounded coyotes. If it thrusts them through with its arrows, great clouds of smoke suddenly arise, and the creatures silently and mysteriously disappear in the air. What becomes of them Me-su-la knows not. Others may take their places. Who knows?

"Mortals cannot tell from whence they have come, nor whither they go. They may increase or they may decrease. It matters not now. They are the enemies of our spirits. Let the warrior thrust his barbed arrows through their vile bodies, and spare never one.

"Fortunately for the spirit of the warrior, the Chiquitos can see no better than mortals, and when the night has come on it can continue its journey without being seen.

"At the first appearance of the spirit, the dwarfs send their runners far ahead in great haste to gather their clans all together, to meet it on the way. Then as the spirit advances, it finds the country before it suddenly covered with its enemies hurrying rapidly towards it from every direction, except that from which it has come, screaming the meantime, like panthers, and howling like wolves.

"Failing in all their efforts to frighten the brave spirit, and cause it to return, they attempt to compel it to go back. Gathering in great masses, they advance to give it battle, attempting to protect themselves the meanwhile, from the weapons of the spirit, by means of their ears, outstretched like the wings of great birds, cooling their heated bodies when the sun shines upon them.

"As the Chiquitos come near, they utter loud screams, and dart their short spears, and shoot their sharp arrows in clouds, while some among them, more brave than the others, fall down upon the ground and await the approach of the spirit, to wound it as it passes. All day long the fight is continued, and the smoke of the wounded Chiquitos mark the trail of the spirit as it slowly presses forward on its journey. At last the sun disappears, and the welcome darkness puts an end to the fierce battle, and forever ends all the trials of the victorious spirit.

"The soft light of the morning scarcely falls on the trail of the spirit before it arrives on the shore of a great lake of water, beyond which not even its far-seeing eye is able to reach. The water shines in the early sun like polished silver, and the pebbles on the shore are brilliant as stones that burn of themselves in the dark, and are never consumed.

"While the spirit stands gazing upon the clear beautiful waters, a canoe made of sweet-smelling cedar, ornamented with silver and great shining stones, comes quickly towards it. A beautiful woman, tall and slender, her face white like the snow when it falls, her long hair bright as the sun when it rises from the mountains, her shoulders half covered by a beaded blanket, far richer than any in the Nation, stands in the canoe, and as it reaches the shore, calls to the spirit to come.

"The woman is the beautiful Nah-wish-to, the queen of the country of the dead.

"She takes the spirit in the canoe, and returns quickly again, over the great silver waters, to her home on an island.

"The beautiful squaws, who have waited and watched a long weary time for the coming of the spirit, meet it on the shore of the island, and taking it up in their arms, bear it joyfully away to their happy ho-gan.

"Ah, me!" sighed the old man, "the heart of Me-su-la is weary with the things of this life, and he would that the

Great Spirit could now permit him to depart for the eternal country of the dead."

The old man had worked himself into a condition of great mental excitement, and when he at last ceased to speak, he threw himself forward upon his robe, and concealed his face with his hands. . To-mé, himself scarcely less excited by the words and the fervor of the oracle, sat silently watching him, not knowing what to say or to do.

He had heard often before a vague legend related in the lodges of his people, of the journey of the spirit through the lands of the dwarfs to the Island of Bliss, but he had never before been fully convinced of its truth. For the first time in his life he had heard it now definitely confirmed from a reliable source, and his soul had been suddenly filled with the ardor of a faith newly awakened. No follower of Mohammed ever more earnestly desired to attempt Al Sirat, than he now desired to attempt the dread journey and meet the evil dwarfs on the way to prove his valor in battle. He forgot for a while even the purpose of his visit to the lodge of Me-su-la, and gazed, enviously almost, upon the form outstretched before him, lest it had entered already upon the journey of the dead.

In a short time, however, the medicine man sat up again on his robe, and looked quietly about him. Every trace of emotion had vanished, and his face wore again its former look of contentment. Turning at length to To-mé he asked quietly.

"Does To-mé wish that medicine be made?"

"Yes," he replied, abruptly, as though suddenly awakened from the toils of a dream.

"The riding horses are all with the herds in the valley, and Me-su-la cannot walk up the mountain."

"Must Me-su-la go up the mountain!" asked To-mé, with some show of impatience.

"Yea, the Great Spirit himself has chosen the place. Three times since the snows left the top of the mountains, the Great Spirit has spoken with thunder, and hurled the lightning from His hand against the same rock. Great broken pieces lie scattered about, in the shape of a creature with wings. Here Me-su-la must go to make medicine."

"Send quickly to the herd," said To-mé, " and bring the horses to the lodge."

"It shall be done, even as To-mé desired," replied Me-su-la, and calling a peon, he sent the man in great haste for the herd.

When the peon had gone To-mé walked out of the lodge and stood watching him as he ran down into the valley. The herd had wandered away to a great distance from the lodge, and considerable time would necessarily elapse before it could be brought back again. To-mé glanced uneasily at the sun, already low in the heavens, and then down again into the valley. He moved back and forth impatiently for a while, and then suddenly hurried back into the lodge.

"The herd is far away in the valley," he said, "and the sun is near the earth. To-mé must ride to the great council chamber before he can sleep. He cannot wait longer for the horses to be brought. He will carry Me-su-la on his back up the mountain."

Stooping down as he spoke, he lifted the old man up on his back and hurried at once up the side of the mountain with his burden. Arriving at length near the mysterious spot, he placed the medicine man on his feet and retired for some distance down the mountain again. He would gladly have remained to witness the ceremonies of the medicine maker, but Me-su-la almost angrily bade him move quickly away. Stopping behind a great rock not very far distant, To-mé climbed hastily to its top, and under cover

of the overhanging foliage of a tree which grew near it, he
watched the old man and listened to hear what he would
say.

The broken masses of rock among which the medicine
man conducted his ceremonies were in full view, but they
served often to conceal him as he moved hurriedly about
from one place to another.

In a short time a little column of smoke, heavily
freighted with the odor of sweet smelling herbs, ascended
from a fire that the medicine man had kindled at his feet.
As the smoke enveloped his person he began to gesticulate
with his arms and to move his head and his body to and fro
in a violent manner, chanting the meantime without intermission, in a low, monotonous tone. At last he suddenly
brought his incantations to a close, and clasping his head
quickly with both of his hands, stepped hurriedly aside
from the smoke.

The words which he should speak as a medicine man had
"come into his head" while under the influence of the
pungent odor of the herbs, and he had held them there
with his hands until the supernatural power which inspired
them had taken its departure.

The medicine was now made, and the old man apparently
well pleased with his work, quietly extinguished the fire
and coming out from the sacred place called To-mé to approach. Once more the runner took the old man upon his
back, and in a short time returned him again to his lodge.
Not a word had been spoken concerning the result of the
medicine making, but To-mé felt well assured by the smiling face of the medicine maker that it had been to the full-
est extent all he desired.

"Will Mu-su-la ride with To-mé to the great council
chamber?" he enquired at length. "The woman will be

there with her daughter, and the medicine man can speak
to Po-lone the words in his mouth.''

''Yes, Me-su-la will ride and he will speak to the woman
the words in his mouth, and To-mé shall have the maiden.
The heart of the warrior will be glad for a while, but sad
days will come quick to his ho-gan.''

All the necessary preparations were soon made for the
journey, and the medicine man and the warrior rode away
together, followed presently by two or three squaws and
several peons, driving before them a small herd of horses.
Their progress was necessarily slow on account of the feeble-
ness of the aged Me-su-la, and it was late in the night when
they arrived at the mouth of the cañon. Choosing a retired
spot near the rocks at the base of the mountain, they quickly formed their encampment.

As soon as To-mé had dismounted he placed his horse in
the care of the squaws, and hastened on foot towards the
camp-fires of the clan of Mariano. As he approached the
encampment he observed the woman Po-lone, standing not
far away, watching a group of warriors sitting about one of
the fires.

''Ah!'' he murmured, ''the woman is anxious to know
that To-mé has returned.''

The thought that the woman was anxious about his return, gave him great pleasure, and he started towards her
at once. He had approached quite near and his lips were
already parted to speak when it occurred to him suddenly
that he might possibly be guilty of some new indiscretion if
he should trust himself to address her. Turning quickly
about he moved rapidly away, as though fleeing from some
imminent danger, and returned hastily to the encampment of
the medicine man.

''Have the feet of the warrior run away with his head?''

asked the old man impatiently as To-mé suddenly made his
appearance again.

"Yea," he replied hesitatingly, "To-mé is afraid of his
head and has brought it quickly away. Me-su-la must hasten to speak to the woman," he added hurriedly. "Even
now she wanders about among the fires in the encampments,
searching for To-mé."

"The warrior must have patience," said the medicine
man. "Me-su-la is weary and must lie down to rest.
When the sun drives the shadows from the valley again, he
will speak to the woman."

"Nay, nay," urged the runner, "To-mé is afraid of his
head and cannot now be patient. The back which bore the
medicine man up the mountain to-day is never weary and
can bear him again."

Stooping down suddenly he took the old man up on his
back without even asking his permission, and carried him
away rapidly toward the encampments.

When he came near the woman's camp-fire, he quietly
placed the Medicine Man on his feet and then hastened
away and secreted himself in the darkness.

He had scarcely disappeared when Po-lone returned from
her fruitless search for To-mé, and seated herself at her
fire. Here the old medicine man found her as has already
been told, and accepting her proffered invitation, cast his
blanket aside and sat down on her robe.

He bowed his head for a time, after the manner of the
medicine man, and at last looking up, spoke briefly "the
words in his mouth." When he had concluded he arose to
his feet and walked slowly away, and soon disappeared in
the darkness.

To-mé hastened to meet him, and taking him again upon
his back, carried him speedily to his encampment.

VII.

At the first dawn of day, the squaws and the peons began to move about in the encampments. As they got out of their blankets they called noisily to each other and then hurried to the places where the horses were tethered, and soon could be heard wrangling among themselves, and scolding at the animals that had become entangled in their fastenings.

The warriors were speedily awakened by the noise, and turning impatiently in their robes, grumbled at the "loose-tongued" peons and squaws.

In the meantime the herds were rapidly gathered together, and speedily despatched to the pasture grounds in the valley. The camp fires were quickly rekindled and the squaws began to prepare the morning meal for their masters and themselves. Blankets and robes were then carefully folded and lashed in convenient parcels, to be carried on the backs of the animals, and all other necessary preparations successively made to remove with the least possible delay from the encampments.

A removal was by no means expected or intended, but the habit of making daily preparations for a change of location, had long been encouraged by precept, and often enforced by necessity, until it had become a recognized and imperative duty, among these nomadic people. Day after day, as regularly as each morning succeeded, these preparations were rigorously renewed. Under no circumstances, however urgent, could they be dispensed with or delayed. In the village, as well as on the journey, in the winter, as well as in summer, at all times and under all circumstances, these

preparations were made, as invariably as the days succeeded
each other. As a people they were ever ready to resume
their traditional wanderings, or as individuals to straggle
about on the slightest provocation.

At an early hour in the morning the runner To-mé made
his appearance riding rapidly across the great plain from the
East. He proceeded at once to the mouth of the cañon,
and announced to the watchman the speedy approach of the
principal men of the clan of the head chief Barbon-ce-to.
A moment thereafter a great horde of mounted savages rode
suddenly into view, from a narrow pass in the mountain,
away to the east of the cañon, and galloped at full speed
across the great plain.

In the absence of Barbon-ce-to, a venerable, old, grey-
headed warrior, rode steadily in front, acting as chief of the
clan. He brought his caravan down to the mouth of the
cañon, and halting it there, dismounted from his horse as a
mark of respect to his chief. Barbon-ce-to himself hastened
to the side of the old warrior, and assisted him to mount
again on his horse, and then returned to his place by the
side of the watchman. As soon as he was gone, the old
warrior wheeled his followers about, and to the great disappointment of the spectators, and the young bloods of the
clan, proceeded at once to the spot selected for his encampment.

One clan after another, now came riding down from the
North, headed by the most renowned warriors of the nation.
Each clan as it arrived, proceeded directly to the mouth of
the cañon, where its leader dismounted in token of respect
and submission to the authority of the head chief of the
nation.

The displays of horsemanship which succeeded each other
almost without intermission during the remainder of the

day, varied but little from the displays made by the clan of
the war chief Manu-le-to.   There was no cessation, however,
in the interest taken by the constantly increasing crowd of
spectators.   The women and peons gathered together in
large, noisy groups and expressed their delight at the ex-
ploits of their favorites, by clapping their hands, or rubbing
them industriously together.   Indifferent performances and
failures were treated with silence.   Not a word indicating
censure was heard, and but seldom a loud word of praise.

The warriors stood apart from each other, wrapped in
their blankets, and witnessed the displays without evincing
in any manner, except 'by their presence and attention, the
least sign of interest or concern.   They remained for hours
at a time standing motionless and erect, like statues carved
from the rocks on which they stood.   Not a single act, however, escaped their observation, and when they gathered together at night in groups about their fires, and dismissed
the conventional' silence that had enslaved their tongues
during the day, they talked glibly enough of every chief
and his clan, and of every horse and his rider, and praised
or condemned, as worthy critics do the world over.

Long established custom had made it the exclusive privilege of the chiefs of the clans to proceed to the meetings
of the great council accompanied only by such prominent
persons as they chose to honor by a formal invitation.   The
trail of a chief could not be followed by those who had not
been especially invited, until the sun had ceased to shine
on it.   Usually, on the morning following the departure of
the chief, large numbers of the people, principally the
younger members of the several families of the clan, set out
in great haste for the encampments at the great council
chamber.   As these people successively arrived they took
their places at the rear of the line already formed by the
chief and the principal men of the clan.

About midday the party of Utes that had caused the alarm on the preceding night made its appearance on the plain. It was preceded by a messenger, "carrying tokens of peace in his hands, and words of friendship in his mouth."

Advancing to the entrance of the cañon, the messenger dismounted and approached the head chief and took him by the hand. Barbon-ce-to received him with a great show of friendship, and so soon as the usual conventionalities were completed, extended an invitation to the party to join the encampment of his clan.

The messenger rode away presently, highly gratified with the result of his mission. In a short time he returned, followed by his party, and after the usual formalities of respect were accomplished, led it to the rear of the clan of Barbon-ce-to where it speedily formed its encampment.

As the sun disappeared behind the mountains to the west of the plain, the representative men of the last clan arrived. So soon as the necessary formalities were completed, they gathered around their chief and hurriedly formed their encampment near the mouth of the cañon.

The chiefs of all the clans with their principal men now had arrived, and Barbon-ce-to looked down from his place by the side of the watchman, with pardonable pride, upon the vast encampment at his feet.

A hundred brave warriors had gathered at his call, followed by a vast retinue of peons and squaws, and an immense number of horses. A thousand more valiant braves could have been assembled, if he had commanded their presence. In his simple imagination there existed nowhere in all the broad land so powerful a people as his own, none certainly whose warriors were so brave, or who excelled them in the practice of all manly deeds. In all the long cata-

logue of desirable things, not one existed which his people
did not already possess. Every virtue was practiced, and
every time-honored custom was observed. His warriors
were intrepid and truthful, invincible in war and loyal in
peace. What more could a great chief desire?

His measure of happiness was full to overflowing. He
considered himself the most favored of all mankind, and
would have scorned, doubtless, the richest crown in all chris-
tendom, in exchange for his honors.

At a late hour of the day the common people began to
make their appearance, and before the sun had gone down,
the plain was dotted here and there with individuals and
parties, approaching from every possible direction.

As darkness came on they signaled their arrival by shouts
and peculiar loud cries which were often recognized and answered from the clans to which they belonged. The shouts
of the warriors, the boisterous merriment of the squaws
over the newest arrivals, the neighing of the horses, and the
yelping of the wolfish dogs that prowled in common herds
about the encampments, produced a scene of confusion seldom witnessed among these habitually stoical people.

At last, sometime near midnight, the people ceased to arrive. The neglected camp fires burned low, flickering occasionally here and there with little tongues of flame, before they went out altogether. The noise died entirely
away, and the encampment eventually, was shrouded in silence and darkness.

At an early hour on the following morning, Barbon-ce-to
called the chiefs of the clans, and the principal men into
the great council chamber. As they successively arrived,
they seated themselves in a circle about the head chief, and
waited in silence for the formal opening of the council.

After these dignitaries had all passed through the narrow
opening into the cañon, great numbers of the common

people followed, and seated themselves about the circle of the chiefs and the principal men.

When the noise and confusion caused by the entrance of the people had in some measure subsided, Barbon-ce-to arose in his place, and with impressive deliberation addressed the chiefs of the clans.

"My brothers," he said, "twelve days have passed since the head chief sent out his runners to invite the chiefs of the clans to meet him in council.

"Every chief has responded and the heart of Barbon-ce-to is glad.

"For himself and his people he bids them all welcome."

The head chief presented a remarkably fine personal appearance as he addressed these words to the council. He stood before it a full head in height above the common stature of his people, and straight as an arrow from his quiver. His manners were free from restraint, and his address courteous and pleasing.

His people regarded him with reverence and affection, and his influence over them was unbounded. By his counsel and authority, the nation had been kept at peace with all of its neighbors, so far as was possible, for a long period of years, and had consequently enjoyed great prosperity, and had grown largely in numbers and power.

When Barbon-ce-to had completed his opening address, the war chief Manu-le-to arose, and advanced slowly towards him, with the token in his hand which he had received from the runner.

"My brother," he said, addressing the head chief, "three days have now passed since Manu-le-to rode away from his hogan on the waters of the Cariso. There the runner of the head chief found him, and gave him this token. The heart of Manu-le-to was glad, because the head chief had spoken, and he hastened to meet him in the great council chamber.''

When Manu-le-to had concluded his address he stepped forward hastily and returned the token into the hands of the head chief.

One after the other, the chiefs of the clans, now arose in their places, and gave an account of the arrival of the runners at their ho-gans, and expressed the great pleasure it had given them to respond to the invitation to meet their brothers in council. Each chief advanced immediately upon the completion of his speech and returned the token he had received into the hands of the head chief. When this ceremony was completed, Barbon-ce-to again addressed the chiefs of the clans.

"My brothers have ridden a long distance and are weary,'' he said. "Shall the head chief speak the words in his mouth, or shall he wait until his brothers have grown strong again?''

He dropped his head on his breast, and waited for a reply. A short silence ensued and then a venerable old chief arose in his place and in slightly tremulous tones slowly responded:

"Nay, my brother, the hearts of the chiefs and the principal men of the nation never grow weary, and their ears are always open to hearken to the words of Barbon-ce-to. Let him speak now.''

When the aged chief had concluded his response each warrior in the circle nodded his head in approval of his words. Thus encouraged, Barbon-ce-to proceeded again.

"My brothers,'' he said, "the heart of the head chief is glad, because the Great Spirit has permitted the nation to become the most powerful of all people that live on the earth.

"From a small beginning, it has grown very great. From a small stick that trembled in the wind, it has become a great tree that laughs at the storm.

"Once it was a child, but now it is a man.

"Once all the people hid themselves from their enemies, because they were few. They built their ho-gans on the sides of the mountains where the eagles make nests, for they were afraid.

"Now the warriors hide themselves no more, and rejoice when their enemies are seen.

"They build their ho-gans in the valleys. They are as the rain drops in numbers, and their hearts always are strong.

"Once all the nation gathered together in the great council chamber. Now the chiefs of the clans, and the principal men almost fill the vast place.

"Are not the words true, that Barbon-ce-to has spoken?"

The chief ceased to speak, and bowed his head on his breast. A murmur of voices immediately arose, and the chiefs and the principal men nodded their heads to express their approval of the words they had heard. When this anticipated response had been made, Barbon-ce-to resumed his address.

"My brothers," he said, "hearken to the words of the head chief.

"The nation is great, because it has long been at peace. It is mighty, because it has not wasted its strength needlessly in war.

"The voice of Barbon-ce-to has been heard in many councils pleading for peace. His voice has not changed from the first. The same words have been always in his mouth.

"Has Barbon-ce-to been any the less brave, because he desired peace for his people?

"Is there a warrior in the nation who can say that the heart of Barbon-ce-to has not always been strong?"

The chief spoke almost fiercely, and his eyes burned while he glanced rapidly about him. His auditors sat motionless and silent while he looked enquiringly and defiantly in their faces.

"It is well," resumed the chief, after a brief pause. "The nation has been at peace, and has grown very great. The voice of Barbon-ce-to has been heard always pleading for peace, and his heart has been strong. There is no one to say nay.

"My brothers, hearken well to the words of the head chief.

"If the evil days should ever come on the nation when war must be made, then the voice of Barbon-ce-to will be heard in all the land, calling upon the chiefs of the clans to lead their young men to battle.

"Are not the words of Barbon-ce-to all good?"

Again the chief paused for a reply, and again a murmur of voices arose among the people, and the chiefs and the principal men nodded their heads, even more vigorously than before.

"My brothers," continued the head chief, "hearken to the words of Barbon-ce-to.

"A great war-path leads from the council chamber to the North. There are no traces of blood yet upon it, nor broken arrows to mark its evil course. The grass grows green yet upon it, and hides it from view. Flocks of sheep feed quietly upon it, and are not yet disturbed.

"This great war-path waits for the ready feet of the warriors.

"At the first battle cry, the flocks and the grass will disappear, and then whitened bones and dry withered roots will soon take their places.

"Let the council make haste to destroy this great trail, or to send the young men upon it.

"The herds of the Utes have eaten grass in the valleys of the nation, and the herds of my people have been hungry.

The Utes had hot words in their mouth when they came, and they called the valleys their own.

"Is there better cause to be found for the battle cry of the warriors? Shall not the nation defend its ho-gans?

"Barbon-ce-to will answer for his people. He need not stop to ask them what he shall say. His words will make the hearts of the young men rejoice.

"For this purpose, he called the chiefs and the principal men of the nation to meet him in the great council chamber. He bade his runners make haste with the tokens that he placed in their hands. He counted the days of their absence, and watched with impatience for the coming of the clans. They are here. The chiefs and the principal men are before him, and his heart is now glad.

"My brothers, two days have passed since a messenger came from the head chief of the Utes with words of peace in his mouth. The herds of the Utes have been driven from the valleys, never again to return, and horses will be given to my people for the injury they have received.

"The face of Barbon-ce-to was hot from his anger before the messenger came. Now it is cool, and he is ready to listen to words that are wise.

"The great medicine man of the nation has spoken in the ears of the head chief. 'Peace,' he said, and then was silent. Barbon-ce-to bade him speak yet again, but he had no more words in his mouth.

"The heart of Barbon-ce-to was sad when the medicine man spake, and he sat in his lodge until the sun had gone down, and moved not in his place until it shone in the valleys again. Then his heart became glad because the Great Spirit was kind, and had kept his people from war.

"Let all the chiefs speak. Has Barbon-ce-to been wise, and are all his words good?"

The chiefs and the principal men bowed their heads gravely, and the people remained silent.

"It is well," resumed the head chief. "There shall be peace with the Utes. Barbon-ec-to has spoken. There are no more words in his mouth."

One after the other the chiefs of the clans now arose in their places and addressed the great council. The great interest which had been awakened by the speech of the head chief soon entirely disappeared, and the people gave indifferent attention to the formal speeches that followed. They talked in subdued voices among themselves, and shuffled about uneasily from one place to another.

Among the chiefs there were a few speakers who were noted in the nation for their eloquence. They expressed their views always with vigor, and illustrated their ideas by pantomime, that all understood, and by familiar scenes drawn from nature. The people waited with impatience for the time when one of these notables should rise to his feet.

At last the great war chief Manu-le-to, renowned among his people no less for his eloquence than for his skill as a warrior, arose slowly to address the great council. The murmuring voices of the people, and the shuffling sound of their feet upon the rocky floor of the chamber, ceased instantly and profound silence ensued.

"Nay, brothers," said the chief. "Manu-le-to has but few words in his mouth.

"The medicine man has spoken, and the words of the head chief are all good. Why should the war chief trouble the council with more words?

"There is peace in the land, and words should be few and well chosen. War, like a cloud, hangs always on the border of the nation, ready to drift on the clans.

"War is the common custom of all the tribes beyond the
nation, and the nature of all things that the Great Spirit
has made. Tribe wars with tribe, and one warrior with another. The young men are destroyed, and the old men are
wearied with watching.

"The beasts in the mountains kill each other. The
birds in the trees, and the fish in the waters destroy one
another.

"The fierce wind fights the mountain in its way, and
drives the earth from its top into the valley. It hurls the
sand against the rocks, and eats holes in their sides. The
grass dies in the shade of the trees, and worthless weeds eat
out the rich pastures.

"An old man from the far away country where the sun
first appears, came once to the ho-gan of Manu-le-to. There
was war among the tribes in his land, and the old man was
weary.

"A chief among his people came to the ho-gan of Manu-
le-to from the shore of the great water, where the sun disappears. His people were at war with all the tribes near
them, and made their homes in the cañons.

"A few of the young men of the nation have journeyed
across the land of the Utes, and gone far to the North.
All the tribes in the North are at war, and the people suffer for food.

"Manu-le-to has journeyed for many days to the South,
where the snow never falls, and the sun shines hot on the
ground. The tribes at the South are at war, and the people eat insects and roots.

"My brothers, there is war in the country where the sun
rises. and in the country where it sets. There is war in the
North, and there is war in the South. There is no peace
anywhere, but in the land of the nation.

"My brothers, the Great Spirit is kind. The nation is at peace, and it is strong. If war comes, it must come to make peace. The nation will send her young men on the war-path, and fight to make peace.

"Manu-le-to has spoken. There are no more words in his mouth."

When the war chief had concluded his address, the people at once began to converse with each other in low in distinct tones. The chiefs and the principal men, twisted about un-easily in their places, and nodded their heads vigorously. Several minutes elapsed before order was in any manner re-stored, and the noise sufficiently abated to enable the coun-cil to proceed.

There was but one chief among those yet to speak, whom either the chiefs or the people desired to hear. This chief was Mariano. He had obtained a national reputation for the eloquence of his language and the wisdom of his words in the councils of his clan, and an unusual curiosity had been awakened to see the young chief, and hear his address.

He had never yet stood before the great council, and with the majority of the people his reputation rested upon common report. There was therefore a strong desire to hear what he would say, and how well he would say it.

At last after a long period had elapsed, made weary by in-terminable, prosaic speeches, the young chief arose to address the great council.

"My brothers," he said, "Mariano is the youngest among the chiefs of the nation, and his clan is the smallest. His words have not yet grown very strong, and they may not reach the ears of the chiefs of all the great clans.

"Mariano comes from the South, where peace is not known. The wild Apaches on one side, and the hated Mex-icans on the other, stop not on the war path to hearken to words that are wise.

"The neighing of stolen horses, and the cries of captive maidens, are sweeter in their ears than all the wise words of peace.

"The great council cannot change either the nature or the customs of these people. The strongest words of the chiefs will be hurled at them in vain. They laugh at words that are wise, and despise the warriors who use them.

"They howl like famished wolves about the lodges of the clan, and twang their bow strings in defiance.

"My brothers, Mariano once saw a bear in the mountains pursued by hungry wolves. They snapped and snarled at him and when he turned slowly upon them, they hastened away. He growled wisely at them, but because he pursued them not to their hurt they turned upon him again more quickly than before. They tore his flesh with their teeth and vexed him with wounds. Then he turned quickly upon them and followed them at last to their hurt, and they fled from him sore afraid and left him in peace.

"My brothers, Mariano once saw an eagle flying low along the valley pursued by birds with swift wings. At last the eagle turned for his life and followed his enemies wherever they went until his beak was made red with their blood. Then he flew away alone and in peace.

"My brothers, the nation must send its warriors to pursue its enemies to their hurt or there can be no peace.

"The Apaches and the Mexicans, and the Utes if need be, must be pursued and sorely punished, even as the bear and the eagle pursued their enemies to their hurt, or there can be no peace. Their ho-gans must be burned, their flocks must be scattered and their herds must be destroyed, or there can be no peace. They must be taught to fear the coming of the warriors of the nation, even as the evil spirits fear the coming of the light, or there can be no peace.

"My brothers, the nation is very great and its warriors are all brave. Its chiefs are all wise and their words are all good. Why should more words be spoken?

"Let the nation defend its ho-gans with more arrows and less words.

"Mariano has spoken. There are no more words in his mouth."

Immediately upon the conclusion of the speech of the young chief, a great confusion arose among the people. They began at once to talk with each other in loud, boisterous voices, and in great apparent excitement. Many of them arose to their feet and pushed their way here and there, gesticulating wildly, and talking incessantly. No civilized assembly could ever have been more thoroughly disorderly than this savage convention now had become. It fairly rivalled for a time the beggarly court of the poor King Pétaud, or the mad parliament at Oxford.

Some of the younger warriors drew their knives and brandished them defiantly over their heads. Others twanged their bow strings and shouted the battle cry. The chiefs remained seated, but many of them gave abundant evidence that they shared the excitement of the people. They moved about uneasily in their places, and nodded their heads vigorously in every direction.

The head chief sagaciously permitted himself to drift with the current, and bowed his head repeatedly, to express his approval of the words of the young chief. When this concession was observed by the people they ceased their noisy demonstrations, and at length quietly resumed their places about the circle of the chiefs.

All of these dignitaries now having spoken, one of the principal men arose in his place, and proceeded to deliver an address to the council. His speech soon proved to be prosaic in the extreme, and his auditors, one after the other,

ceased to give him their attention. The chiefs even, whose
duty it was to give a patient and attentive hearing to every
one who should speak, were scarcely able to conceal their
indifference. The speaker could not fail to observe that
the council had closed its ears against him, but custom had
made it his privilege to speak, and he therefore continued
his address, hoping against fate, that he might yet be able
to say something which would be acceptable to his hearers.
But he was doomed to disappointment. He expressed the
most radical views, without awakening even the slightest
enthusiasm. He offered a solution of the subject under
consideration, which he assured the great council was most
conclusive and important, without even eliciting a look of
inquiry. He advocated a relentless and uncompromising
war against all the enemies of the nation until they were
utterly annihilated, without even securing an encouraging
nod from the most blood-thirsty of all the advocates of the
war-path. His speech at last came to an end, and he sat
down in his place, having failed to obtain the recognition he
coveted.

He was followed by a warrior, who spoke briefly, and
closed a conventional address with an expression in favor of
peace.

Thus, one after the other, the principal men succeeded
each other, repeating for the most part, almost to the echo,
the words of one or the other of the popular speakers who
had preceded them.

When all of these representative men had been heard,
Barbon-ce-to again arose to address the great council, and
close its proceedings.

"My brothers," he said, "the chiefs and the principal
men have spoken for their clans.

"Their words have been good, and the heart of Barbon-
ce-to is glad.

"The head chief will speak for the nation. His words will make the hearts of the old men rejoice. The young men will be glad.

"These are the words of the head chief. He speaks not for himself. He speaks for his people.

"There shall be peace with the Utes, and war with the Mexicans and the Apaches. There shall be wise words for the tribes in the North, and there shall be barbed arrows for the tribes in the South.

"The herds of the Utes must come no more upon the pasture ground of my people. The warriors of the Mexicans and the warriors of the Apaches, must come no more into the country of the nation.

"The great council is ended. Barbon-ce-to has spoken. There are no more words in his mouth."

As soon as Barbon-ce-to had concluded his address, the chiefs and the principal men arose to their feet, and without further ceremony began to file slowly and silently out of the great council chamber. After all the chiefs and the principal men had passed out, the people began rapidly to follow, moving forward one after the other, and pushing impatiently through the narrow opening out on the plain.

A long time elapsed before the last of this restless procession reached the entrance of the cañon. The sun had already disappeared behind the mountains when the last individual passed out, and dark shadows were rapidly gathering. Behind him the great council chamber was shrouded in darkness, and loathsome vampires and hideous owls had already come up from the unknown region beyond, and startled the echoes anew with the clashing of their wings and their strange, dismal voices. The dreaded spirits of evil were gathering in the great council chamber with unseemly haste to hold their vicious orgies and work evil to the nation.

VIII.

The great council had ended, but there appeared to be no disposition on the part of the people to break up the encampments. The herds were driven to the pastures at the usual hour on the following morning, and blankets and robes were carefully folded and tied together in bundles with the deliberation common to every day life.

The affairs of state had been settled to the apparent satisfaction of all, and there was no further necessity for the presence of the chiefs. But a time-honored custom existed of continuing the encampments after the conclusion of the council, for a short period of feasting and dancing, and general enjoyment. It was evident that this custom was now to be observed, and that the people were about to indulge in a grand holiday occasion. There was to be racing of men and of horses, and exhibitions of strength and of skill. There were to be games of chance, for robes and for blankets, and for buttons of silver and brilliant stones. There was to be buying and selling, and changing of goods. In short a veritable fair and an unceremonious festival occasion.

At an early hour of the day a great crowd gathered about the encampment of the Utes, to examine the robes and the blankets which the strangers desired to exchange, and to look at the horses they had brought from the North to astonish the nation by their beauty and speed. One of these animals had been tethered to the shaft of a lance, that had been driven in the ground near the encampment of the Utes. From the top of the shaft a red ribbon now floated lazily in the breeze, as a challenge for a race.

The conditions upon which all games and races depended

were indicated by a display of symbols and signs, of well known significance. All articles which were to be jeopardized by the result, were publicly exhibited, and usually attached in some way to the lance from which the challenge was floated. No words were ordinarily found necessary to supplement the conditions indicated by the signs, or the services of judges required to settle disputes.

The runner, To-mé, pushed his way through the crowd and stood quietly for a while among his companions, looking at the beautiful animal that was tethered to the lance. At last he stooped down and began slowly counting the number of pebbles displayed at the foot of the shaft to indicate the distance of the race. As he laid the last one aside a warrior near him enquired softly.

"How many, my brother?"

"Five hundred," he replied, and turning about quickly, he walked hurriedly away. In a short time he returned, leading his horse after him, and again approaching the lance, he seized the red ribbon and tore it from its fastenings.

To-mé, with his usual impetuosity, had accepted the challenge. He had acted in a spirit of bravado, rather than from any decided conviction that he would be successful. The warriors of the nation who were rich in fine horses, had not shown any disposition to accept the challenge of the strangers, and To-mé, piqued by the want of spirit they displayed, had determined to set them a worthy example, even though he should suffer the loss of his horse.

One of the Utes came forward at once and unfastened the horse, and drew the lance from the ground. The two warriors then walked together out over the course leading their horses behind them, and counting their steps as they went. When they had reached the distance indicated by the pebbles, the Ute thrust the lance in the ground, to mark the end of the course. Turning immediately about, they walked rapidly back to the encampment.

In the meanwhile the Utes were busily engaged in offering wagers of blankets and robes, upon the result of the race. There appeared to be no probability, however, that it could terminate otherwise than in favor of the strangers, and none of their offers were therefore accepted.

To-mé was more indignant than ever, when he returned from the end of the course, to learn that not even one poor little wager had been made by his friends. Seizing his blanket, he tore it from his shoulders and threw it upon the ground as a wager. It was immediately covered by a robe of great value and beauty, and the two were suffered to remain where they fell, to await the result of the race.

All was now ready, and the riders hastily mounted their horses.

"Go!" shouted a voice from the crowd, and instantly the horses sprang away on the course.

To-mé's horse was unusually fleet, and for a time the two animals ran closely together, without any perceptible advantage to either. The people had expected to see the strange horse dash immediately ahead, and eventually win the race with great ease. To their great surprise and intense gratification, they observed that the horses were apparently well matched, and that the race promised to be close. They clapped their hands incessantly, and shouted until they were hoarse.

"Go on, To-mé! Go on, To-mé!"

"A horse to wager that the runner will win," cried a voice n the crowd.

"A horse to wager that the woman will loose," replied a warrior.

"Go on, To-mé! Go on, To-mé!" still shouted the crowd.

"To-mé will win! To-mé will——."

The cry died away in an incomplete sentence. The Ute had suddenly shot far ahead and was rapidly closing the race. To-mé was struggling hopelessly after, each moment falling farther behind. The crowd ceased its clamor, and looked on in silence, awaiting the apparently inevitable result.

"Po-lone was hasty, and has lost her wager," cried the warrior exultingly.

He had scarcely spoken when the horse of the Ute stumbled forward in his flight, and fell headlong to the ground. The animal rolled over and over in a great cloud of dust that immediately hid him and his rider from view. To-mé shot ahead in an instant, and as he dashed past the lance that marked the end of the course, he drew it from the ground and waved it in triumph over his head.

To-mé had won.

Fortunately, neither the Ute nor his horse had received any material injury from the fall, and the great crowd of people united in a shout when he again mounted his horse and rode forward to join the victorious To-mé.

As the two warriors approached the encampment the enthusiasm of the people increased, and they pressed forward eagerly to meet them. The riders moved on through the crowd to the end of the course, and then the Ute slowly dismounted and surrendered the posession of his horse. This was the signal for shouting again, and To-mé rode away with the robe and the horse he had won, amid a perfect ovation of cheers and much clapping of hands.

By this time little red flags were flying from the top of lance staffs in every direction, and the people quickly dispersed in search of some new excitement.

Shouts could be heard in all the encampments, and men could be seen running and jumping and riding, for wagers, or pleasure, or fame.

Noisy groups gathered in places about athletic wrestlers, and swayed uneasily to and fro, as the struggling contestants forced each other from one point to another.

Eager crowds collected at times about each lance staff that floated a challenge to learn the conditions of the contests proposed and examine the wagers that were offered.

Warriors exhibited their skill in the use of their weapons, in friendly contests with each other, and shot their barbed arrows and hurled their tomahawks and knives with wonderful precision. Others exhibited remarkable feats of strength, and hurled great stones from their hands which an ordinary warrior could scarcely lift from the ground.

In every direction there was something of interest to be seen, and crowds of good humored spectators jostling each other in common, anxious to express their delight and approval at every opportunity. A great free day had come for the people, without discrimination of rank or position, and the chiefs and the warriors, and the squaws, and the peons, mingled promiscuously in the crowds, and bantered each other as opportunity presented, for trials of skill or the hazard of wagers.

Immediately after the conclusion of the race between To-mé and the Ute, the woman Po-lone hastened away to receive the horse she had won, and place it in charge of her peon. After she had accomplished this purpose she spread a robe on the ground near her encampment, and seating herself upon it, she began shuffling a pack of strange looking cards with great skill and ostentation. Close by her side, some rich blankets of beautiful patterns, a few buttons of silver, and some articles of use and ornamentation, were displayed.

The cards that she held in her hands had been cut from the thin skins of young kids and trimmed to a uniform size with a knife. They were almost circular in shape and had been cut with such exactness, that a difference could not be detected in their size or their thickness. They were painted with images of chiefs and of warriors, and of beasts and of birds, and inanimate things, to represent different values.

Po-lone shuffled them about from one hand to the other with remarkable dexterity, and soon attracted a crowd to witness her performance.

At last she threw a large button of silver on the robe and shook the cards at the spectators as a banter to play. The people nodded their heads and challenged each other to try their fortunes with the cards. A warrior presently threw a button of silver by the side of the wager and sat down on the robe. Then another warrior sat down, and finally two squaws followed their example and seated themselves on the robe and cast down their broad pieces of silver.

Po-lone laid down the cards as a signal that the lists were now closed, and that the game would begin. The warrior who sat next her took up the cards and shuffled them nimbly for a moment and then passed them to the next player in the circle. This process was accomplished successively by each of the players and the cards were then carefully replaced on the robe in front of the woman.

Taking them up quickly, she snapped off the top card by a nervous motion with her hand. She turned the card over and revealed to the eager view of the players the picture of a beast. Casting the card before the first player on her right, she again snapped off the card on the top of the pack and exposed it to view. It was marked with the image of a bird, and was cast before the next player in turn. The beast was stronger than the bird, and the first card was the best.

Again she snapped off a card from the top of the pack and exposed it to view. It bore the image of a chief. The spectators at once expressed their delight by a shout, and the squaw who received the winning card clapped her hands nervously and chuckled with joy over her good fortune.

"Bah!" cried Po-lone. "The squaw already counts one."

As she spoke she thrust her hand in a pouch that hung at her girdle, and drew out a beautiful white pebble of transparent quartz and placed it before the squaw to mark her first winning.

Again a card was snapped off from the top of the pack and the picture of a bird was exposed.

"The chiefs go much together," exclaimed the squaw who had received the last card. "Why do they come alone from the pack?"

"The chiefs mingle with the people on free days," answered a voice from the crowd.

"Bah!" cried Po-lone, as she drew a card from the top for herself and exposed the picture of a warrior. "Bah! If the chief had not come, the warrior would have been best."

Again the same process was repeated and each of the players was served with a card. Two birds were thrown down and a beast proved victorious. The holder of the beast received a white pebble to mark his success.

A third time the cards were dealt off, and a warrior fell before the squaw who had won the first count, and she received another pebble.

A fourth time and a chief again fell before her, bringing her third winning and the possession of the wagers.

"Me-ra!" she cried exultingly. "The words of the squaw were all good. The chiefs go much together. Two came from the pack and fell at the feet of Sin-ma-tula."

She rubbed her hands industriously together, and indulged in a low chuckling laugh over her chiefs and her three winning pebbles.

The spectators were vastly amused at the earnestness of the squaw, and laughed loudly at the extravagant display which she made. At last she gave back the cards and the pebbles to the woman, and gathering together the five broad buttons of silver, she fastened them slowly, with trembling fingers, to her girdle.

Again Po-lone cast down a wager, and each of the players covered it at once with a similar article, or with others of similar value. The cards were then shuffled by the players in succession, and the game proceeded as before. Po-lone was the winner this time, and when the game closed she quietly gathered the cards all together, and drew her winnings towards her without exhibiting the least evidence of emotion.

One game now followed another in rapid succession, the greater share of the winnings finding their way to the dealer. The good fortune of the squaw Sin-ma-tula deserted her after the first game had been played. The chiefs fell no more at her feet. The birds and the beasts even refused her the small hope they could bring, and losing cards only now fell before her. She continued, however, to play, stimulated by the hope that her good fortune might eventually return. After each successive loss, she placed her hope upon the venture to follow, and hastened each time, more eagerly than before, to cast down her wager. One after the other, the five pieces of silver that she had fastened at her girdle were successively ventured and lost.

At last she ventured her blanket, the work of her own skillful hands, over which she had toiled day after day, for a whole year, to weave and embroider. A considerable time was necessarily consumed in the selection of articles that she was willing to accept as fair wagers against her rich venture. When all this preliminary work was arranged, a pile of great value lay before her, with ten horses at least, from the best herds in the nation. Choice robes of rare animals and handsome fabrics of wool lay one above the other, and numbers of great broad buttons of silver, partially concealed by the folds of the robes and the fabrics, glistened in the sun like imbedded jewels. But the blanket of the squaw, beautiful because of its exquisite texture, the symmetry of its interwoven figures, and its richly embroidered edges, was most conspicuous of all the many object in the pile.

The spectators looked on in silence, and the players sat in their places, immovable as statues. The cards went around at length, from one to the other, and after much nervous shuffling and many meaningless ceremonials and abracadabras said over them to influence a fortunate result, they were at last returned to the woman.

To the delight of the people who thronged about the players, the squaw Sin-ma-tula won the first count. She rubbed her hands joyfully together and chuckled aloud over her good fortune.

Again the game proceeded, and cards marked with chiefs and with warriors, and with beasts, and with birds, and with inanimate things, fell before the players in rapid succession. The spectators jostled each other and pressed closer together in their eagerness to witness the play, and when at length the squaw again was successful they gave expression of their sympathy for her by a shout.

The squaw now held two pebbles to mark her two winnings, and her final success appeared well assured. None of the other players had yet now a count, while she had but one more to make.

The game went on immediately again, and the best card came next to the woman. She helped herself quietly to a pebble 'from her pouch, and again dealt the cards to the players. Once more the best card fell before her, and she again won a count. Her chances for final success were now equally good with the squaw. Probably indeed they were better, for she was expert with the cards and, from some cause or other known best to herself, she was usually successful when the wagers were large.

A warrior won the next count and by a strange coincidence won immediately again. Then his brave companion received the best card, and after him the squaw who sat by the side of Sin-ma-tula.

Again the cards were carefully shuffled in the same manner as before, and the woman snapped them off spitefully one after the other, and threw them down on the robe. A losing card was the first, and then came a beast. A warrior followed next for the squaw Sin-ma-tula, and a bird succeeded for the squaw who sat by her side. A card was yet to be removed from the pack for the woman, and the issue of the game rested entirely on its value. Po-lone ceased to snap the cards from the pack, and, with great deliberation removed one for herself and extended it before her. She averted her face that she might not see the card as she turned it over slowly with her hand and let it fall on the robe.

So soon as the face of the card was exposed to the view of the players, the squaw Sin-ma-tula uttered a deep groan, and a low murmur of voices immediately arose in the crowd.

Po-lone at once understood the significance of these sounds, and, turning her head quickly about, looked at the card. It bore the image of a chief. The rich wagers, the blankets and robes and the broad buttons of silver, were now all her own. She slowly drew them towards her without evincing the least sign of emotion, and placed them at her side with her previous winnings.

Poor Sin-ma-tula bowed down her head and remained silent. No one about her knew the extent of her grief. She had sat down at the game possessed of many valuable articles of personal use and adornment. The last one was gone, and she was now utterly impoverished and wretched.

Po-lone hastened to put an end to the scene, and casting a silver button upon the robe hurriedly offered it as a wager. Her challenge met prompt response from all of the players, except from the squaw, who still sat in her place with her head bowed on her breast, and her face hid in her hands.

"Will the squaw again venture a wager?" enquired Po-lone.

"Nay," she replied, uncovering her face and raising her head. "Nay, Sin-ma-tula has nothing left now to venture."

"Another wager might win," said one of the warriors, "and the squaw soon again would be rich."

"Sin-ma-tula has nothing left now but herself," she replied.

"The services of the squaw for a moon, would be a fair wager against a button of silver," suggested Po-lone.

"Nay," cried the squaw with great animation. "Nay, a button of silver is but a small thing, and a moon is soon passed. Let the woman wager the blanket that once was Sin-ma-tula's."

"And what will the squaw wager?" asked Po-lone.

"Sin-ma-tula will wager herself for twelve moons against the blanket," she replied, desperately.

The players nodded their heads, and hastened at once to make offers of wagers of equal value with the blanket. When this had all been accomplished to the satisfaction of the squaw, Po-lone carelessly cast the blanket upon the pile, and passed the pack to be shuffled. The cards passed around the circle as before and were at last returned to the woman.

Sin-ma-tula was the first to win a count and immediately thereafter the squaw who sat by her side was equally fortunate. Then one of the warriors won twice in succession, and Po-lone after him won also a count.

The spectators had apparently lost all sympathy for the infatuated squaw, and they looked on in silence to witness the result of her last rash venture. They had not long to wait. The warrior who had already two pebbles now won again, and the squaw, and the blanket, and the other rich wagers, were at last all his own. With cruel haste he at once ordered the squaw to go to his encampment in the clan of the war chief, Manu-le-to, and wait there until he should come.

The poor creature sat motionless like one in a daze, until her new master in a peremptory voice bade her "begone!"

She had scarcely gotten up from her place when a squaw elbowed her way through the crowd to sit down on the robe.

"Nay," cried Po-lone, who had caught sight of a familiar face in the crowd. "Nay, let the squaw wait for a while. The runner, To-mé, desires to play and he shall have the place of Sin-ma-tula."

"The woman is kind," said the runner, "but To-mé will not take the place of the squaw. Fleet horses are better than cards, and trials of strength and of skill are more to his liking."

IX

To-mé walked rapidly away from the group of card players and hastened towards the encampment of the Utes. As he drew near it he observed that a red flag again floated from the top of a lance to which a poor old horse had been tethered.

He could scarcely believe what he saw, and for a short time fully doubted the sincerity of the Utes in flying a challenge to the nation to run against so indifferent a champion. It was evident at least, he reasoned at length, that they intended to accomplish some trick. Possibly, though, they believed that the running horse he had won in the morning had been so severely injured by his fall that it would prevent his appearance again on the track, and so dared to venture in good faith this inferior animal. It would be easy he thought, if such was the case, to teach them a lesson.

Without further reflection he hastily approached and tore the flag from its fastening. Then bidding the Utes await his return, he hurried away for his new running horse. He returned presently, leading the beautiful animal behind him, and joining the Ute who had offered the challenge, the two at once led their horses over the track. Then they hastily mounted and at the word for departure, given by a spectator selected for the purpose, the horses bounded away on the course.

To-mé took the lead almost at the start and ran quickly away from the Ute. When he arrived near the end of the track, the Ute under pretense of urging his horse, shouted at the top of his voice, "Sa-loo! Sa-loo!"

Instantly the intelligent animal ridden by the runner slackened his speed and turned from the track. All the

efforts of To-mé to compel him to go on proved utterly useless. In the meantime the horse ridden by the Ute ran
forward at fairly good speed and at last reached the end of
the course.

To-mé struggled manfully while hope yet remained, to
regain control of his horse. He gave up at last and permitted the animal to follow along passively behind the victorious Ute.

As they drew near the crowd of spectators that had gathered to witness the race, the Utes greeted their companion
with shouts and loud clapping of hands, but the Navajos
looked on in silence.

"The running horse is well trained," said To-mé, bitterly,
as he delivered him up to his former owner, "and the Ute
has won by a trick."

"Nay," replied the Ute, "my brother knows not how to
ride the fleet-footed Sa-loo."

"Hist!" cried To-mé, testily, "let not the Ute call a
Navajo, brother. The meanest warrior in the nation would
despise to play the trick which the Ute has just played, not
even to win the beautiful Sa-loo."

"The words of To-mé are hot," replied the Ute, and
turning about he walked quickly away towards his encampment.

"Is the Ute a squaw?" cried the passionate To-mé, "that
he should run away with hot words in his ears."

Drawing his knife from its sheath as he spoke, he
flourished it over his head and hastened at once in pursuit.

The Ute stopped immediately and also drawing his knife
stood waiting the approach of the runner. One instant
more and a desperate conflict would have doubtless begun,
involving more in the end then a mere personal encounter.

The Utes would have hastened to the assistance of their
champion, and the Navajos to the support of their hot-

headed champion. Such a conflict could only have ended
in the total destruction of the Utes, and then all the wise
words which the head chief might utter, and all his great
influence for peace, would have been of little avail to avert
a relentless war between the two nations.

Fortunately a chief of one of the great clans hastened
from among the spectators at this critical moment, and in-
terposed his authority to restrain the impetuous To-mé.
In a short time quiet again was restored, and To-mé was
hurried away by his friends.

But a brief period, however, had elapsed when he again
made his appearance, leading after him his own faithful
horse, and carrying a lance in his hand, to which a red ribbon was attached. Approaching the encampment of the Utes,
he thrust the lance in the ground and hastily tethered his horse
to the staff. Then quickly removing his moccasins from
his feet, he cast them on the ground at the foot of the lance.

The Navajos at once understood for whom this challenge
was intended, and although there were many fleet-footed
warriors in the nation who would ordinarily have been glad
to lay a wager with To-mé on the result of a personal race
with him, they now stood quietly aside waiting to see the
outcome of the challenge which he thus ostentatiously offered to the Ute.

The strangers themselves comprehended fully the purpose
of the challenge, and they drew hurriedly together in a
group by themselves, and conversed busily with each other.
It was evident to them that the irrepressible To-mé would
force them from one contest to another until he had established his superiority in some particular direction, or had
been signally defeated.

The Ute was a tall muscular fellow, and one of the fleetest
warriors in his tribe. He felt perfectly confident of his

ability to contest successfully in a personal race with the runner, but at the same time he feared that victory would be more disastrous to himself and his companions than defeat. For some time he was in doubt what course to pursue; but finally, acting on the advice of his people, he determined to accept the challenge, and win the race if he could.

The conference of the Utes caused some delay, and the Navajos who had gathered to witness the result of the challenge, became quickly impatient, and at last began to indulge in taunting expressions and shouts of defiance.

"Where is the Ute," cried one, "who wins by a trick?"

"He has gone to his ho-gan," replied another, "to saddle a horse for his squaw."

And then there followed a shout and a laugh and much clapping of hands.

Finally the Ute approached the group, leading behind him the running horse Sa-loo. Without looking to the right or the left, he proceeded hurriedly to the lance and violently tore the ribbon from the staff. Then, fastening his horse to the lance, he announced that he was ready to run upon any terms which the Navajo might name.

The signs that were displayed at the foot of the lance indicated that the race should be made for a hundred paces, and then back again to the point of original departure. The runners were required by the symbols displayed to stop for an instant on arriving at the further end of the course before the return should begin.

To-mé made no response to the boastful offer of the Ute to concede him more favorable terms, and the necessary preliminaries were speedily arranged.

A Navajo and a Ute immediately proceeded to measure the distance to be run, and then each one placed a large stone to mark the end of the course. All now was ready, and a spectator was named to give the word for the start. "Go!" he shouted, and instantly the men sprang away. They ran handsomely together until near the farther end of the track, when the Ute sprang suddenly ahead, and first reached the stone which had been placed by his companion. He stood erect upon it for an instant, and then, stooping down to gather his strength for a tremendous effort, leaped suddenly forward. Unfortunately for him, the stone upon which he stood was not sufficiently large nor well enough imbedded in the ground to afford a good hold for his feet. As he sprang forward it suddenly gave way and he fell heavily to the ground.

In the meantime, To-mé, who had run steadily forward, carefully husbanding his strength, reached the stone which had been placed by his companion, and standing upon it for an instant, sprang heavily away, and sped past the prostrate Ute towards the first starting point on the course. In a moment his antagonist sprang to his feet and leaped forward again. It was evident, however, that the Navajo had acquired a considerable advantage by the fall of the Ute, and as he came on, maintaining his position several paces in advance with much apparent ease, his friends cheered him forward with shouts and encouraging exclamations.

During the early part of the race, and while the advantage all rested with the Ute, his companions cheered him on and clapped their hands in great glee over the prospect of an easy victory for their champion. They now became silent and anxious and looked on with gloomy faces and muttered among themselves against the ill fortune that so persistently attended them.

In the mean time, the two runners were coming back on the course in fine style and rapidly nearing the end of the race. To-mé was straining every nerve now to maintain his advantage, and the Ute was slowly but surely closing the gap that existed between them. At last they reached the end of the course and To-mé sprang across it barely a pace in advance of his powerful antagonist.

His victory had scarcely been accomplished when several of his companions rushed forward, and raising him on their shoulders, bore him about through the crowd with prolonged shouts and cries of exultation. The horses were then unfastened from the lance to which they had been tethered, and the lariats were handed to To-mé. His companions immediately hastened away, bearing their champion upon their shoulders and followed by a great crowd of people. They passed rapidly through the encampments of several of the clans, shouting almost incessantly, and uttering loud cries in honor of the brave runner To-mé.

"This is the warrior," they shouted, "who ran a race with the Ute, and who has won fairly the beautiful Sa-loo, the running horse from the north."

After some time had been spent in this extravagant display, To-mé was permitted to mount his horse and ride away from the crowd. He proceeded at once to his encampment, taking with him the animal he had won, and which was now rendered doubly precious in view of the great honors which his victory had brought.

The sun was already low in the heavens when To-mé reached his encampment, and the shouts of the crowds and the tramping of busy feet as the people hastened from one place to another had all nearly ceased. The herds could be seen quietly returning from the pastures, and little fires were already burning here and there throughout the several encampments. The groups of card-players had long since dispersed, and the little red flags which had fluttered defiance from many lance staffs in the morning had now all disappeared. The races and the games and the contests had all ceased for the day.

The old medicine man met the runner with warm expressions of kindness, and, sitting down on a robe, bade To-mé take a seat by his side and tell him what notable things had occurred.

"To-mé will speak to Me-su-la," said the old man, "and tell him how well the young braves can shoot and how well they can ride, and who among the warriors has won the most praise."

"To-mé's heart was made glad," he replied, "by the honors he received. He has won the running horse, the beautiful Sa-loo, which the Utes brought from the north."

"To-mé has done well," said the old man. "Let him keep his running horse and venture him no more. The day will soon come when To-mé's heart will be glad because his horses are fleet. Let him break his lance now, and tear his red flags in pieces, and close both his eyes and put his fingers in his ears, until the Utes and all the people have gone."

"The words of the medicine man are all good," replied the runner.

"To-mé will speak again to Me-su-la," said the old man, "and tell him the name of the warrior who was borne through the encampments upon the shoulders of his comrades to-day."

"To-mé's comrades bore him upon their shoulders," he replied.

"Bueno!" exclaimed the old man, musingly. "Then the words of the woman were true. The brave To-mé has won the most praise."

"The woman?" asked To-mé, hurriedly, "why came she to the encampment of Me-su-la?"

"Po-lone is in trouble," the old man replied, "and she came to Me-su-la with sad words in her mouth."

"Will she obey the good words which the medicine man has spoken," asked the young man anxiously."

"Yea, the woman will obey," replied Me-su-la, "but she asks that medicine may once more be made, and if the words in the mouth of the medicine man are the same as before she will come herself to the ho-gan of To-mé and give back his promise and the girl shall go to his lodge.

"Nay!" cried the impetuous To-mé, springing quickly to his feet. "The words of the woman are not good. The medicine man has once spoken. He should not speak again."

"If the words of the medicine man were all good," replied the old man, "the Great Spirit will put the same words again in his mouth. Let the warrior have patience."

"Nay! nay!" cried To-mé. "The Great Spirit may grow weary. Let Me-su-la make medicine no more."

"Me-su-la has promised," he said, "and he will make medicine once more."

"Me-ra!" shouted the runner with great violence, as he walked excitedly to and fro. "To-mé will gather together his friends and——."

"Hist!" cried the old man angrily. "Loud words travel far and reach many ears. To-mé's head is hot now because he has heard words of praise from his comrades to-day. His mouth has grown large quickly because he has won a horse from the Ute. Let To-mé look upon his feet that they lead him not into trouble. The customs of the nation are good every one and they must all be obeyed."

The old man ceased to speak and looked inquiringly at To-mé, as though he waited a reply.

The runner continued for a time to walk to and fro, but at last he stopped abruptly and raising his clinched hand turned quickly towards the medicine man. His face bore a grave, resolute expression and his eyes burned fiercely.

"Hist!" cried the old man again. "Let not To-mé speak while his head is yet hot. His words cannot be wise until his head has grown cool."

"To-mé has many friends," he said defiantly, scarcely waiting until the old man had finished," and they will come——."

"Nay, nay," pleaded the old man. "Let the brave To-mé think once again before he speaks evil words."

"To-mé has no time to think," he replied. "He will act first and think after." And turning quickly about he walked rapidly away.

"Let To-mé look well to his feet," shouted the old man after him, "that they lead him not into trouble."

To-mé had not gone very far when he stopped quite abruptly, and turning about once more approached the medicine man.

"The last words of Me-su-la did not all reach To-mé's ears," he said, "and he has come back again that Me-su-la may speak them once more."

"The heart of Me-su-la is glad," said the old man. "To-mé went away like a jabbering squaw. He has come back like a warrior. When To-mé's head is hot," continued the oracle, "he should turn his face to the wind and count the pebbles in the sand. A hot head is never wise, and swift feet are foolish."

"Me-ra!" cried the hunter, with a gesture of impatience. "To-mé came not back to hear new words in the mouth of the medicine man.

"Me-su-la has new words in his mouth," replied the old man, "that To-mé will be glad now to hear. Let the warrior sit down on the robe and open his ears that Me-su-la may speak softly. The wind cannot keep a secret. It carries words like a squaw."

To-mé stood irresolutely for awhile marking figures on the ground with the toe of his moccasin. At last he slowly came nearer, and eventually sat down on the robe.

"Has the medicine man many words in his mouth?" he asked hurriedly.

"Nay, Me-su-la has but few words in his mouth," replied the old man, "and they will soon all be spoken. Are the ears of To-mé open?"

"Let the medicine man speak."

The old man drew nearer to To-mé, and, after looking cautiously about, began to speak in an almost inaudible tone and with great deliberation.

"To-morrow," he said, "when the sun shines on the tops of the lodges, the woman will break up her encampment and ride with her daughter and her herd for the ho-gan of Me-su-la."

"Nay!" cried To-mé, violently. "the woman will not ride to the ho-gan of Me-su-la."

"Hist!" whispered the old man. "The winds are made glad when To-mé is angry. They laugh when they hear his strong words."

"To-mé will listen," he said hurriedly. "Let the medicine man speak again."

"To-morrow when the sun shines in the tops of the lodges," continued the old man, "the woman will break up her encampment and ride with her daughter and her herd to the ho-gan of Me-su-la. Then after medicine has been made, she will ride to the south on her way to her ho-gan on the bank of the Puerco. To-mé must ride before her until her journey is done."

"And why must To-mé ride before the woman?" he enquired.

"The Apaches might meet her on the way," replied Me-su-la.

"Apaches!" cried To-mé, eagerly. "Where are they? Who has seen them? Let the medicine man speak quickly."

"Hist!" again whispered the old man. "To-mé must cease to talk to the winds, or Me-su-la will find no more words in his mouth."

The runner bowed his head submissively and remained silent.

"A peon came from the ho-gan of Me-su-la," continued the old man, "while To-mé's companions bore him on their shoulders through the encampments to-day. Some horses have been stolen from the herd and strange moccasin tracks have been found in the valley where the herd had been pastured."

To-me sprang quickly to his feet and tightened his belt and gathered his blanket hurriedly about him.

"Where does To-mé go now?" asked the old man quietly.

"Quick to the head chief," he replied, "and then to the ho-gan of Me-su-la. To-mé will ride with the war party that goes in pursuit."

"Let To-mé turn his face to the wind," said the old man with provoking deliberation, "and think for a breath. What if the horses have strayed and the moccasin tracks have been made by a grizzly monster from the mountains? The peon is not a warrior."

A long silence ensued after the old man had spoken, broken only by the hard breathing of the runner.

"The words of the medicine man are wise," he said at length in a subdued manner. "The words of the medicine man are all wise," he repeated. "It is best to think first."

Then dropping his blanket upon the robe, he sat down again in his place.

"To-mé will hearken to the words of Me-su-la," he continued after a brief pause. "Let the medicine man speak again."

The old man made no reply, but calling a peon to approach, he ordered that a horse should be quickly saddled and brought to him. The peon hastened away and in, a short time returned with the horse. By the assistance of the young warrior the old man mounted the animal and seated himself in the saddle. Then turning towards To-mé, he leaned forward and whispered softly in his ear.

"Me-su-la rides to the encampment of the head chief. To-mé will watch the fire while it burns until he rides back again."

Without waiting for a reply he rode slowly away towards the mouth of the cañon, followed by the peon on foot.

To-mé seated himself upon the robe, and waited with impatience for the return of his friend.

A beautiful autumn day had just closed. A gentle invigorating breeze, scarcely strong enough to carry a dried leaf from the mountain to the plain, had prevailed from the early morning.

The hazy atmosphere, common to the great plains and the valleys of this elevated region at this season of the year, had partially obscured the bright rays of the sun, and intercepted the heat. The Great Spirit had smiled upon his children, and given them this evidence of his care and protection.

But as the sun had descended behind the great ragged mountains to the west of the encampments, the Great Spirit had temporarily withdrawn his protection, and the gentle breeze had been quickened by some evil agency into a great rushing wind, which now swept down upon the plain with great violence, burdened with the moanings of the disturbed spirits that made their abode in the forest on the side of the mountain. Dark clouds from the council fires of evil elfs had been driven up from the bottomless cañons beyond the great mountains, and pushed over the intervening rock-

covered heights, one after the other, until now the whole
heavens were covered, and the fair face of the sky, studded
with the bright fires of the Great Spirit, were hidden entirely
from view.

After the lapse of some time, the wind began to abate
somewhat of its violence, and at last died entirely away.
An oppressive heaviness in the air, and an unnatural still-
ness immediately succeeded.   The black clouds ceased their
flight and hung almost motionless above the encampments,
burdened now with the rain which the Great Spirit had sent
from the great waters, in which the sun sank to sleep at the
close of each day.

· To-mé raised his eyes and peered anxiously into the deep
darkness above him. The thought that the trail of his thieving enemies would be obliterated by the rain which was threatened, and their pursuit thereby rendered impossible, served
further to increase his impatience and anxiety.

As he sat looking at the clouds, a single drop of rain sent
by the Great Spirit as a messenger to foretell the coming
storm, fell upon his face and confirmed his worst fears.

But almost at once an expression of great resignation came
over his anxious, uplifted face.

The Great Spirit had spoken in the little rain drops that
had fallen upon his face, and he had accepted unreservedly
the message implied.

"The Great Spirit is wise," he said thoughtfully, and all
that He does must be good.   He is kind to His people.   He
speaks to His children and they hearken to His words."

When he had finished his invocation, he bowed his head on
his breast and remained for some time in silent communion
with the Being he worshipped.

He sprang at last to his feet and hastened to arrange his
robes and his blankets under an arch made of sticks and of

brush by the squaws of the medicine man. When he had completed his work, he spread a great robe over the top of the arch to protect him from the rain and fastened it securely in its place.

A similar structure had been erected and carefully covered by the squaws for the use of their master.

The old man now made his appearance, riding slowly into the encampment, followed by the peon on foot. He was assisted to dismount and then proceeded at once to his bed. Stopping for an instant on the way, he turned his face towards To-mé, who stood the meanwhile near the fire waiting patiently for the old man to speak.

"Me-su-la is tired," he said, in a low, weary tone. "He will speak the words in his mouth when the sun shines again on the plain."

X.

A bright, beautiful morning dawned upon the encampments. The clouds had all passed away and many traces of the storm had already disappeared.

To-mé sprang from his bed at the first dawn of light and wandered listlessly about the encampment. His face bore an expression of composure and perfect resignation as he stood watching for the first rays of the sun. But as the light slowly increased and his fears became more fully confirmed, he found it impossible to conceal his disappointment. He looked out upon the great, broad valley before him in utter despair. Not a single track or a trail of the many that had existed on the previous day, could now be seen. The face of the valley had been ruthlessly washed during the night by the rain, and every foot-mark upon it had been completely destroyed.

The faith of the young warrior in the wisdom of the Great Spirit was for the time sadly shaken, and he was almost upon the point of rebellion against his previous convictions.

"The Great Spirit is wise," he murmured, "and all that He does must be good. But why," he continued more earnestly, "should He hide the vile enemies of the nation under dark clouds and wash out their trails with the rain?"

"Yea, yea," he continued after a brief pause, speaking rapidly as though he hastened to atone for the doubt expressed by his words. "The Great Spirit must be wise, for He has made all things, and they are all very good. To-mé has but little wisdom to understand what the Great Spirit has done or why He has done it."

"But To-mé is wise a little," he added after another brief

pause, speaking this time more slowly and with a somewhat injured air, "or he would not understand that the work of the Great Spirit is good. Why then can he not understand a little of all things that are wise?"

"The young savage had almost reasoned himself into the belief that his own created faculties could exercise supernatural powers, and that he was now either arbitrarily deprived of this advantage, or that the acts of the Supreme Being were unwise. His own strong, untamed and undisciplined will had intervened to awaken these doubts and destroy his faith and his peace. He had interpreted the falling of the drop of rain on his face, as he had impatiently looked into the sky on the evening before, as a personal message sent direct from the hand of the Great Spirit, foretelling the inevitable rain and demanding from him a patient submission.

Even this small recognition had filled his heart with great gratitude and wonder and had awakened a faith that had given him great comfort and peace at the time. The Great Spirit had spoken as literally and impressively as though a voice from the clouds had reached him and said: "The Great Spirit speaks. He will do what is best. To-mé must cease to be impatient. The Great Spirit is displeased with those who murmur against Him."

But now that the rain had indeed come and its immediate effects were disastrous to his hopes, so far as he could see, his half formed faith and imperfect submission gave him but little assistance to regard it as all for the best.

He walked away mechanically farther and farther from the encampment, repelled unconsciously by the noise of the squaws and the herds. At last his progress was suddenly arrested by the thought that one hope which he had hitherto entirely overlooked, yet remained. It was barely possible

that the rain had not fallen in the mountains or in the
valleys beyond, and that the trail of the thieving Apaches
or the hated Mexicans, whichever they were, still existed and
would enable pursuit.

He stopped short to think.

The morning air had been cold and he had gathered his
blanket close about him when he left the encampment. He
had failed to notice until now that it had become somewhat
oppressive, and he hastened at once to unloosen its folds
and throw it aside.   As he did so, an enormous tarantula
detached itself from the blanket and fell to the ground.

To-mé sprang back from the repulsive creature in affright,
and watched it with horror as it slowly and defiantly walked
away.   Its spider shaped body was covered with short,
straggling, black hairs that stood up on end, and only partially concealed its snaky looking skin.   Its legs also were
covered with short, black hairs, but of apparently much
softer texture than those on its body, and in much greater
abundance.   The hideous creature was at least two inches
in length and fully half that measure in diameter.   It
moved slowly and laboriously along, dragging its great, baggy
legs as though they were heavy and offered an impediment
to its progress.

These venomous animals were seldom seen in the country
inhabited by the Navajos, and the people therefore knew
but little about them.   This fact however had not in the
least tended to limit common report.   In this, as in most
other cases where imperfect knowledge existed, an opportunity was presented to indulge in the marvelous.

In the course of time, therefore, the most wonderful accounts of these creatures became common and obtained general credence.   They were supposed to be able to spring to
immense distances when enraged, and were seldom or never

killed before they had succeeded in inflicting mortal wounds ,
with their poisonous fangs upon the persons of those who
encountered them. They were naturally ferocious, and the
presence of a human being aroused them at once to the
most intense excitement and extraordinary activity.

The medicine men shook their heads and remained silent
when the creature was named in their presence. They had
no knowledge of any antidote for the dreaded poison from
their fangs, and all their charms and incantations were
popularly believed to be powerless against its deadly effects.
They shook their heads mysteriously and covered their faces
with their hands. The evil spirits had taken full possession
of the venomous creatures, and the wise medicine men held
their peace and kept their own council.

Far away to the south, many days travel over mountains
and plains, these animals were frequently found. A few
brave hunters and warriors of the nation had at one time or
another penetrated into this distant country, and after en-
countering almost incredible dangers and privations, had
eventually returned to their people after long periods of
absence, burdened with most wonderful accounts of what
they had seen. While these intrepid hunters and warriors
remained in this far away country, their lives had been constantly endangered by the hideous creatures, and would
often have been sacrificed but for the virtue of the charms
that they wore and their fleetness of foot. At night they
had often abandoned their encampments when the dreaded
creatures were found lurking near, and during the day had
often changed the course of their march to avoid them.

They were never seen after the first frosts had come until
the warm days of summer returned. Early in the autumn
each one of the creatures constructed a house for its own
occupation during the winter, and when the frosts at last

came it speedily closed itself in and fell into a sleep that lasted until the hot summer sun awoke it again.

These winter houses were each built in a little excavation sunk in the earth deep enough to afford temporary protection and concealment for the structure. As the season advanced and the fall winds began to sweep over the plains, they were speedily covered by the drifting sand and at last concealed entirely from view.

The walls of the houses were constructed of mud and vegetable fiber and erected in a circular form. A small opening was left at the top of each house to admit the body of the builder. This opening was covered by a door constructed from a flexible, gelatinous mass, secreted by the creature and strengthened by hairs and vegetable fiber, skillfully interwoven. It lay snugly on top of the house, completely covering the opening and apparently closing all means of entrance or exit. It was fastened, however, on only one side, where it was joined to the wall by a strong, flexible band that served as a hinge.

When all the exterior work was completed, the creature hastened to finish the interior. With remarkable industry it gathered together day after day the fur and fine hairs which the conys and the coyotes had shed against the bushes of mesquit and the more common bunches of cactus, to line the interior.

It finally completed its work, and when its instinct taught it that the time had arrived to begin its long winter sleep, it retired into its luxurious abode and sealed the door fast in its place.

The creature which had fallen from the blanket of the runner had strayed far from the place of its nativity. Possibly it had been caught in one of the fierce whirlwinds that occasionally sweep over its native plains and had been carried far away into the country of the Navajos, where it had since wandered about in vain search for its well-known haunts.

"Me-ra!" cried the young man joyfully, so soon as he had well recovered from the surprise which the creature had given him. "Me-ra! The evil spirit has now gone away and To-mé is free once again. He whispered evil things in the ears of To-mé and made his heart sore."

He ceased to speak almost abruptly, and for a moment stood looking intently at the animal. Then the joyful expression that had brightened his face died suddenly away, and a look of great determination took its place.

"He must die now," he said resolutely, "even though To-mé must die also."

The young man, with his usual impetuosity, had determined upon a most desperate and hopeless attempt. He had been taught from his infancy to believe in the existence of evil things, possessing supernatural powers, that could be employed to the injury of human beings, or to influence them to their hurt. In the creature before him, he recognized one of the most dreaded of all the malignant forms, in which these evil things presented themselves. It was this hideous creature, doubtless, that had tempted him to rebel against the Great Spirit and to murmur at his good and wise acts. It was better, he reasoned, that he should now lose his life and destroy the evil thing, than that it should be permitted to live to deceive him again, and possibly work other evil in the nation.

Impelled by this desperate purpose, he hastily drew an arrow from his quiver, and, fixing it to the string of his bow, sent it with great force at the creature. The arrow struck on the earth directly beneath it, and threw it violently into the air. It fell upon its feet and hastened away more rapidly than before. The young man instantly fixed another arrow upon the string of his bow, and with his blanket wrapped in a great fold about his arm, to be used as a shield in the final struggle with the creature, hastened on after it.

He had unconsciously taken this useless precaution, against a result which he regarded as inevitable. He anticipated that the creature would be able to inflict a mortal wound upon him in some way, he knew not how, before he could possibly hope to destroy it, or might even assume some other form of dreadful proportions and power, to crush him to the earth and leave him to die upon the plain.

He rapidly drew near to the animal, and at last came so close that it stopped and turned quickly towards him to meet his attack. He instantly sank down on his knees and discharged the arrow with the utmost force he could command. Again the weapon struck on the ground directly under the creature, and threw it with great violence into the air. This time, however, the arrow had struck upon firmer ground than before, and its recoil was much more severe. The animal fell to the ground sorely wounded. It made several vain efforts to rise on its feet, and struggled desperately with its wound. In a brief time its struggles ceased altogether, and before its intrepid pursuer could again discharge an arrow, its lifeless form lay stretched out before him upon the ground.

"Me-ra!" he cried exultingly. "The evil thing is dead."

Then, raising his eyes towards the morning sun, he continued in a low, subdued voice.

"The Great Spirit is good. He made To-mé's arm strong and guided the arrow that wounded the hated thing. To-mé's heart is made glad, and his thoughts are all good."

When he had ceased his devotions, he stooped down where the dead creature lay, and thrust the sharp barb of an arrow through its body. Then, raising it up cautiously, he hastened towards the encampment of the medicine man, carrying it before him.

"What has To-mé on the barb of his arrow?" cried the old man, excitedly, as the warrior approached him.

"Does not the medicine man know?" asked To-me calmly, as he held out the arrow with the creature impaled upon it.

The old man leaned forward on his robe and shaded his eyes with his hand, and looked intently for a moment at the creature.

"Me-ra!" he shouted. "Take it away. Quick!" he added beseechingly, and with hands outstretched. "To-mé hears the words of the medicine man. Quick!" he shouted as he hid his face in his hands. "Take the evil thing away, that Me-su-la may see it no more."

The young warrior instantly threw the creature from his arrow upon the ground, to a considerable distance from the terrified medicine man, and then, turning towards him said quietly,

"The creature is dead. Why is the medicine man afraid?"

"The Great Spirit has gone away," he replied with great agitation, "and the evil spirits have come to do evil work. Good things and evil cannot remain in the same place together. When the evil spirits come, Me-su-la knows that the Great Spirit has gone far away."

"But what has To-mé done?" he added sternly, after a short pause, during which he regarded the young man attentively. "Did he talk with the evil thing?"

"Nay, nay," cried the runner indignantly, "the creature hid in the folds of To-mé's blanket while he slept, and when it had whispered evil things in his ears, it fled from him. The Great Spirit came then after it had gone, and made To-mé's heart brave and his right arm strong, and he followed after the evil thing and killed it when it turned upon him. Has To-mé done wrong?"

"To-mé is brave, and he has done well," answered the medicine man, "and the heart of Me-su-la is glad. But

the evil thing which To-mé has killed was not strong. If it
had been strong To-mé would first have been killed, and
the heart of Me-su-la would be sad."

The old man paused and looked anxiously about him.

"Hist!" he said at length, speaking almost in a whisper.
"Me-su-la must hasten to his ho-gan. Other spirits, more
dreadful and much stronger, may come to do evil things.
The Great Spirit is angry with his people and has taken
himself far away."

Then hurriedly calling his squaws and his peons about
him, he bade them hasten to drive back the herd from the
pasture and saddle the horses and fasten the packs with all
possible speed. So soon as this was accomplished and his
people were mounted, he directed the caravan to move
quickly forward across the great plain towards the mountain in which he had built his ho-gan.

"Shall To-mé ride with the medicine man?" asked
the warrior. "The sun will soon shine in the tops of the
lodges, and the herd must not stop on the way."

"Nay," replied the old man, "To-mé will ride with the
young braves which the head chief will send. He will soon
pass the herd of Me-su-la with his warriors on his way to
the mountains. To-mé can be a great chief if he will—
when he is older. Let him be wise."

When the old man ceased to speak, he was assisted at
once to mount on his horse and immediately set out, following after his people.

To-mé stood for some time in the place where the medicine man had left him, watching the caravan as it made its
way laboriously across the great plain. At last he turned
abruptly aside and walked quickly to the place where his
horses were tethered, and mounting directly rode away
towards the encampments.

"The medicine man is growing old," he murmured impatiently, "and is troubled with fears. He trembles when danger is near, and hastens to hide himself in his ho-gan."

The clattering of horses feet awakened him suddenly from his reverie, and looking up he discovered several young warriors galloping rapidly towards him. When they came near, they reined in their horses, and drew up around him in a group.

"And where rides the brave O-see-to with his comrades to-day?" inquired To-mé, addressing a swarthy young savage among them.

"Wherever the brave To-mé shall lead," he replied. "The horses are fresh, and the young men are ready."

"The heart of To-mé is made glad," he replied. "But why come O-see-to and his comrades to ride with To-mé?"

"O-see-to knows not," he replied. "The head chief has sent the warriors to ride with To-mé. They can tell why they were sent when they ride back to their ho-gans again."

"O-see-to and his comrades are brave," said To-mé, "and if the foot-marks that the peon has found in the pasture grounds of Me-su-la have been made by the Apaches or the Mexicans, the young men will have many words in their mouths when they ride back to their lodges again."

This was the first intimation that the young warriors had received of the purpose for which they had been sent to report to To-mé. Meager as the information now given them was, it seemed entirely sufficient to gratify their curiosity, if indeed they had any at all. At least, not a single question was asked, and the little party rode away presently in silence, following the trail made a short time before by the caravan of the medicine man.

Each warrior of their party led a spare horse behind him, laden with blankets and food. They rode along one after

the other, each followed directly by his own led horse. To
the distant observer they presented a most singular appearance as they moved slowly along across the great plain, following the windings of the new made trail, presenting no
break whatever in the long line made by their horses. Mov-
ng on thus, the picture was almost complete of some mon-
istrous creature crawling steadily forward in pursuit of the
less orderly party of the medicine man.

To-mé cast his eyes on the ground and rode on in silence.
He felt himself greatly aggrieved as he recalled the strange
questions which the medicine man had asked him concerning the evil thing he had killed. Even the peculiar conduct
of the old man had left an impression upon his mind that
it bore a rebuke in some way, he could not well understand
how.

The more he thought of it the more indignant he became.
There was no reasonable doubt left now in his mind, that
the medicine man had thus purposely sought to change the
friendly relations that existed between them, in order that
he might be able to serve the present purpose of the woman,
and save himself, thereafter, from any further importunities.
Settling down finally upon this conviction, he determined to
ride clear of the caravan, and avoid a meeting that could
not be otherwise than painful to himself. Turning aside,
therefore, from the trail he rode away to the right, in the
direction of a prominent spur in the great mountain range
that lay before him upon the Eastern border of the plain.

As the party approached near the broad base of the mountain, it became involved in the foot hills and breaks that
intervened between the mountain and the plain. Many of
these were found entirely impracticable for the animals,
and much time was lost in making necessary changes in
direction. The party at length reached the last foot hill
before it, and slowly ascended to its summit.

Between the mountain and the place where the warriors now stood, a deep gorge had been washed through the rock, by the torrents of waters that for ages had swept down from the mountain during the yearly season of rain. The rocky face of the gorge seemed almost perpendicular, and presented an apparently impassable barrier to all further progress in the desired direction. The horses drew back in affright as they came successively to the brink, aad turned quickly aside or threw themselves back from the chasm.

To-mé sprang at once to the ground, and leading one of his horses as near as he could to the edge of the chasm; forced the animal over. So soon as the terrified beast found its fall was inevitable, it threw out its feet, and bracing itself backward, slid safely to the bottom, a distance of at least thirty feet. One after the other the horses were then brought to the brink and forced over, until the last one had gone down. When this had been accomplished, To-mé and his companions slid quickly to the bottom and once more continued their journey.

The side of the mountain at the place which the party had reached was precipitous and entirely impracticable for the animals. Proceeding, therefore, along the bottom of the chasm it found a comparatively easy ascent for a considerable distance, and at last came out almost imperceptibly upon the rough, weather worn side of the mountain, more than half way up to its forest covered summit. From this point the ascent was easily accomplished, and the party soon reached the broad, level mesa that crowned the top of the mountain. Stopping here, under the wide spreading branches of a great juniper tree, the weary horses were permitted to rest.

After a brief delay had been made for this purpose, the warriors again mounted their horses and once more set out.

To-mé led the way, following close along the edge of the mesa, until he emerged from the forest upon the rock-covered point towards which he had ridden after abandoning the trail of the medicine man. From this point the great valley lay revealed to the gaze of the young warriors. They involuntarily reined in their horses, and sat silently gazing down upon the vast plain that lay at their feet. Away to the North as far as the eye could reach, and far away in the dim distance to the South, not an object intervened to intercept the almost limitless view. Occasionally the great mountain ranges that bordered the plain on the East and the West, sent out ragged spurs and broken foot hills far into the valley. But these offered no obstacle to a full view of the grand scene which presented itself from the top of the mountain.

The sun had just disappeared behind the summit of the mountains to the West of the plain, and dark shadows had gathered at their base. The encampments at the mouth of the cañon were already completely concealed by the darkness.

"Me-ra!" shouted one of the warriors, pointing quickly with his finger at some moving objects upon the plain, "another herd follows the great trail to the mountain."

"The warrior sees the herd of Me-su-la the medicine man," said one of his companions.

"Nay," replied the other. "The herd of the medicine man is already far up on the mountain. The herd on the plain is not the herd of Me-su-la."

"The warrior sees the herd of the woman, Po-lone," said O-see-to slowly, as he gazed fixedly at the object.

"Me-ra!" cried To-mé abruptly. "The sun sinks low behind the mountains. The warriors must ride."

Then hastily turning his horse, he rode quickly away, wed at once by his companions.

XI.

The war party had not ridden far from the rock-covered point where it had halted on the summit of the mountain, when it suddenly emerged from the forest and made its way down into a little grass covered valley, which To-mé presently recognized as a part of the extensive pasture grounds over which the great herds of the medicine man ranged. When he had well assured himself that this was the case, he drew out of the valley and proceeded parallel with it, under cover of the forest that bordered its side. But the rough, broken character of the ground near the forest soon drove him down into the valley again, and compelled him to follow its course. As the party proceeded, the valley became gradually wider, and the forest that bounded it on the East and the West drew slowly away and at last entirely disappeared in the gathering darkness.

A well-beaten trail extended down the valley, and To-mé now determined to find it. He had followed it a few days before with the medicine man on his way back from the South, and he believed it was not far away. He permitted his horse to move slowly forward expecting each moment to find it. He grew impatient at last at the delay thus occasioned, and leaving his companions, rode· in great haste back and forth in search of the trail. Failing to find it as quickly as he expected, he cast the reins from his hand upon the neck of his horse, and permitted him to choose his own way unrestrained. The intelligent animal, apparently conscious of the wishes of his master, turned quickly aside and soon fell into the trail.

To-mé now confidently pushed forward as rapidly as the darkness would permit, with scarcely a further thought of his course. Occasionally he cast his eyes to the heavens to assure himself by the position of the stars, that the general direction of the march to the Southward was maintained, and then relapsed into seeming indifference again.

The warriors followed their leader in silence, one after the other, along the narrow, well-beaten path. Occasionally a startled rabbit sprang from its cover and sped swiftly away, rustling among the dry grass as it went; or a wandering coyote sprang aside from the trail and howled dismally after them until they had gone out of sight. All else, save the light patter of the horses] feet on the trail, was silent as the tomb.

Several hours had elapsed since the party had ridden down into the valley, and many long miles lay behind it. To-mé had recovered from his seeming indifference and now peered anxiously into the darkness, endeavoring if possible, to discover some familiar object about him.

Suddenly he reined in his horse sharply and gazed fixedly before him in utter amazement. A great broken elevation lay in his path, apparently closing his further advance. His eyes burned like diamonds in the darkness while he gazed. In perfect astonishment he sat in his place irresolute and silent.

Could it be possible, he wondered, that he had found a strange trail and been led into some unknown place. No, he reasoned, that was utterly impossible. Rather the mountain had come from its place and sat down before him. Possibly evil spirits were pursuing him to gratify some malevolence they bore him, and had intervened this barrier to annoy and delay him. Certainly he could not be deceived. No mountain range had ever existed before where this one now lay unmistakably before him, its ragged face plainly outlined against the bright sky.

But, after all, he reasoned with himself, it could not be possible that the evil spirits had placed the mountain before him. Such marvelous work could be effected by the Great Spirit alone. Evil spirits might bring disease, and even death to poor mortals, and do many things that were evil, but they were powerless to create mountains or move them.

"Nay, nay," he murmured. "The Great Spirit has moved the mountain himself. He has come again to speak to To-mé."

His horse moved impatiently about and pressed heavily upon the rawhide bit of his bridle to free his head from the hard hand of his master. Absorbed in his changing thoughts the young man unconsciously dropped the reins from his hand, and the horse instantly turned to the left and hastened forward.

"Me-ra!" murmured his rider, as he seized the reins and restrained the animal forcibly. "The horse has turned his head to the east and moves forward as though a herd was before him."

"Hist!" cried a warrior.

To-mé stopped instantly, and leaning forward on the neck of his horse, listened breathlessly.

"Hist!" cried the warrior again.

"Bah!" said To-mé, after a short pause. "The ho-gan of the medicine man stands among the trees, not two flights of an arrow away. The warrior has heard the tramping of sheep in the corral."

Reining his horse sharply about, he rode back to the trail and approached the elevation again.

As he drew nearer than before the rugged outlines he had previously seen melted gradually away until they ceased altogether to exist.

With a great cry of relief the young warrior hastened forward, thankful that the way was not closed as he feared, but excessively annoyed that he had permitted himself to be deceived by a common night *mirage*. Dealing his faithful horse a violent blow, by way of punishment for the part the animal had taken in the deception, he set out at a rapid pace southward, closely followed by his companions.

After an hour's hard riding, he turned his horse to the left and rode across the valley to the forest that lay like a dark cloud on its border. Halting here under a great piñon tree, the warriors quickly dismounted at a signal from their leader, and after removing the packs and saddles from their horses they picketed the animals securely in the rich grama grass that grew luxuriantly about them.

One of the warriors immediately proceeded to a considerable distance from the party and began to pace back and forth along the edge of the forest, watching as well as he was able in the darkness and listening attentively the meanwhile for any indications of danger.

Another warrior quickly gathered some dry cedar bark, and pulverizing it almost to a powder, laid it on the ground and spread over it a quantity of resinous matter that he had detached from the body of the tree under which the party had halted.

When he had completed these preparations he took a small stone from his pouch and holding it near the dry tender, struck it violently with the blade of his knife. Bright sparks of fire fell instantly upon the bark and the inflammable resin, and quickly set them on fire. Little twigs and broken sticks were then gently added until the blaze sprang up at last and burned vigorously.

The warriors had brought with them a considerable quantity of meat that had been provided for the feasts which always attended the meetings of the great council. Each individual of the party choosing his own time, cut out a great slice and laid it on the embers to broil. When they had all satisfied their hunger, they lazily spread down their blankets on the ground near the fire, and one after the other lay down to sleep.

When all was again quiet and the light from the fire could no longer be seen, the sentinel returned to the camp and leisurely broiled a piece of meat over the few coals that remained, watching the meantime attentively about him. At last he got up and wandered slowly and noiselessly about, keeping some distance from the camp, and stopping often to look and to listen. After many hours of this silent watching had passed, the sentinel approached his companions and quietly awakened them. The warriors sprang quickly to their feet and seizing their weapons, glanced hurriedly about them.

"The light will soon come," said the sentinel, softly.

It was yet dark, but the position of the stars and other natural indications with which the warriors were familiar, confirmed the words of their comrade. Comprehending immediately the purpose for which they had been awakened, they noiselessly gathered their blankets and hastened into the valley for their horses. In a short time the animals were saddled and packed and ready to resume the journey again. Mounting at once, the warriors rode silently away, observing the same order in their march as on the previous day.

Almost immediately after their departure, the soft gray light of the early morning began to appear, and the day fully dawned before they were well out of sight of the ground where they had camped for the night. They moved forward rapidly, keeping close along the edge of the valley and under the dark shadow of the trees. Occasionally a single warrior left the party and rode across the open ground

to the forest beyond, or far up into some connecting valley
or cañon, searching the ground thoroughly in every direction. All these precautions, however, proved useless, and
failed to discover the least indication of the presence of the
enemy. Assured by these repeated examinations that the
object of their search could not possibly be near, the party
turned at last into a little open space in the forest where
the horses could be concealed, and dismounted to permit
them to graze. Leaving a single warrior to guard them, the
others hastened into the deep forest near by to prepare their
morning meal.

In the management of his party, To-mé had followed the
customs observed by the renowned warriors of his nation
under whom he had served. The camp for the night was
now made by these redoubtable men of war, until the darkness had enabled them to effectually conceal their intentions. Even then it was often changed from one place to
another, especially when any immediate danger was ap-
prehended.

When the camping ground was finally selected, it was
necessary that the animals should be unsaddled and un-
packed, and that they should be taken at once to some open
place where grass could be found, in order that they might
be permitted to graze. Every warrior regarded the care of
his animals as a paramount duty, and in case of an unexpected attack while in camp the imperative necessity for
their speedy removal to some more defensible place than the
grazing grounds usually afforded. For a time, therefore,
after the enemy had made an unexpected appearance, the
warrior's attention was necessarily divided, and his immediate services largely impaired. To guard against this con-
tingency every available means was employed to conceal the
location of the camp, and to make the delay while in this

partially defenseless condition of as short a duration as possible.

To-mé and his companions had scarcely passed out of sight of the spot upon which the camp for the night had been made, when two half-naked, squalid, ill-favored look- ing savages rouse up stealthily from among the broken frag- ments of a great rock that lay almost within sight of the place, and with bodies half bent and short wary steps, made their way slowly through the forest towards it. When they reached the edge of the valley, they gazed anxiously up and down and looked cautiously about them as though in doubt what had become of the warriors. At last one of the sav- ages discovered the trail of the party, leading to the south- ward along the edge of the forest, and he immediately fol- lowed it for a considerable distance, bending over it and studying it with care, in the vain attempt to discover the strength of the party by the tracks of the animals. Return- ing at length to his companion, he threw himself down on the ground and crawled out in the valley on his hands and knees to the place where the horses had been picketed to graze. Here he was more successful and in a short time re- turned to his companion in the same manner in which he had gone.

"There are seven warriors," he said, "and each has two horses."

"The trail can be followed," said his companion, "and the horses all taken while the warriors are asleep."

"Nay, nay," said the other. "The warriors are on the warpath. They close but one eye while they sleep, and they ride hard on the trail of their enemies. The herd of a squaw party has good enough horses for my brother."

The two Apache warriors were repulsive, vagabondish looking creatures. Their short, ill-fitting buckskin shirts were covered with grease and with dirt. Their moccasins, surmounted by long leggins that reached above their knees, were torn and much soiled. Their long black hair fell unkempt upon their broad shoulders, and their heavy, unwashed faces still retained traces of the paint with which they had been adorned before they had started upon their present expedition. They were short in their stature, and of powerful build; fair representatives altogether of the nation to which they belonged. They presented a striking contrast in their personal appearance to the tall, well-formed and graceful Navajos, in their comparatively clean, well-fitting garments of deer skin and wool.

The Apaches crouched down in the midst of a thick growth of bushes that grew near the trail, and glanced restlessly about them like wild beasts alarmed by some threatened danger of which their senses had apprised them. After waiting for some hours in this concealment for the coming of the herd of the woman or the medicine man, which they had discovered from some hiding place on the previous day, they finally stole noiselessly away and disappeared in the forest.

After a brief delay had been made To-mé again caused his warriors to mount and once more pushed rapidly southward. As he proceeded, the forest trees that grew on either side of the valley, gradually became more diminutive in size and fewer in number until at last they ceased altogether. The valley itself terminated suddenly upon a great mesa, almost entirely destitute of all vegetation or of any object that could afford concealment for the party.

To-mé at once recognized the mesa as the one over which he had ridden but a few days before, when on his way from the encampment of the young chief to the lodge of Me-su-la.

Halting his party under the cover of some stunted piñon trees that skirted the edge of the mesa, he sent a single warrior forward to look down into the cañon at the foot of the mountain.

The warrior rode quickly away and in a short time reined in his horse and dismounted near the brow of the mesa. Cautiously approaching the brink of the precipice, he looked down into the yawning chasm below. Far away to the right and far away to the left for many weary miles, the view of the cañon and the valley into which it opened was almost entirely uninterrupted. On the opposite side a dense forest of pine and enormous masses of rock covered the sloping face of a great broken mountain.

The warrior gazed long and earnestly down into the cañon and into the forest beyond, in the attempt to discover some evidence of the presence of horses or men. Not the least indication of a living thing could be seen, and the warrior turned slowly about to signal to his companions. He hesitated for a moment, and then instinctively turned and once more looked down in the cañon.

Could he be mistaken?

He threw himself quickly down on his face, and barely raising his head from the ground drew his body nearer the brink.

A solitary Apache warrior was moving out stealthily from the cover of the forest. He proceeded directly to the spring that flowed from the base of the precipice, and after slacking his thirst returned again slowly to his concealment, turning about often as he proceeded to cover up and obliterate the tracks he had made in the earth.

As soon as the Apache had disappeared in the forest, the Navajo drew slowly back to a considerable distance from the brink and at last sprang to his feet. Hastening at once to his horse he quickly led him some distance away, and tethered him securely behind a great growth of cactus to effect his better concealment. Returning again to the brow of the mesa, he hastily threw himself down on his face and awaited with anxious suspense the further movements of his enemy. His vigilance was soon rewarded by the appearance of several warriors moving quickly across a small opening in the forest visible only from his elevated position. This revelation was sufficient to convince him that his enemies were seeking for a place of concealment from which they might be able to operate with advantage against the encampment that a party of Navajos returning from the great council, might make in the vicinity of the spring.

He strained his eyes in the attempt to catch another view of the Apaches, but the forest had swallowed them up and hid them completely from his view. Suddenly a single warrior again emerged from the forest and crossed over the cañon, stopping and turning about often as he proceeded to obliterate his tracks. Arriving at last on the opposite side, he ran nimbly along near the base of the precipice upon the loose stones that had fallen from its face, and at last began to climb up the wall by the same trail that the runner To-mé had followed some days before.

"Ah!" murmured the warrior to himself, as he observed his enemy climbing the trail. "The Apache is kind. He hastens to bring up his scalp to hang at the girdle of Ka-nee-no."

Then drawing back from the brink, until far enough away to escape observation from the Apaches concealed in the forest, he raised himself up on his feet and ran quickly to a point near the end of the trail on the brow of the mesa. Throwing himself again upon the ground he crawled forward until within a few feet of the brink, and concealed himself behind a small pile of stones that had been raised by the herders from the village to mark the trail, down which they were accustomed to drive their flocks from the pastures beyond the mesa to drink at the spring in the cañon.

Ka-nee-no had not long to wait for the appearance of his enemy. A black bushy head slowly emerged above the level of the mesa and remained motionless for a time, while a pair of dark, wicked-looking eyes wandered restlessly in every direction over the plain. Assured at length that the mesa was deserted, the wily Apache slowly drew himself up, and at last stood upon his feet and walked back and forth ' near the brink, gazing alternately out on the plain and down in the cañon.

The Navajo watched him fixedly as he moved to and fro, and waited with bent bow and poised arrow until he should get farther away from the brink, and if possible out of sight of his comrades, who might be watching from their place of concealment in the forest. At last the favorable moment arrived, and instantly the sharp twang of a bow string resounded through the air and the Apache warrior, shot through the body by the iron barbed arrow of the valiant Ka-nee-no, fell heavily forward upon the gronnd.

With a low cry of triumph the Navajo sprang forward, and drawing his knife hastily from its sheath, struck savagely at his prostrate foe. To his intense astonishment the wounded Apache suddenly revived from the death-like shock which the wound from the arrow had given him, and, raising his arm, dexterously warded the blow. Then, grappling desperately with his assailant, he dragged him to the ground and struck him heavily with his knife.

The young warrior struggled with all the strength of despair to effect his release from his powerful foe, but all his struggles were in vain. The Apache held him powerless in his grasp, and, raising his knife, slowly poised it for a blow, his fiendish eyes dancing with delight while he delayed the moment of his triumph. The undaunted Navajo glanced at the bright blade as it gleamed above him in the sun, and then, quickly gathering his fast failing strength, nerved himself for a last desperate struggle. The Apache anticipating the attempt of his enemy, tightened his grasp upon him spasmodically, and with almost superhuman strength held him even more firmly and helpless than before. It was but for an instant however. A tremor suddenly seized upon his powerful frame, and his iron hand slowly relaxed its rigid grasp. His raised arm fell powerless to the earth, and the bright bladed knife that he had with unintentional mercy delayed in its course, to minister to his passions, fell from his nerveless hand and rattled harmlessly upon the stony brow of the mesa.

With a low moaning cry he fell forward upon his face in the agony of death. Ka-nee-no perceived that the grim monster had come thus unexpectedly to his assistance; but fearing that the powerful Apache might again possibly revive, he thrust him violently away and instantly plunged his knife to the hilt in his breast. The Apache gave a quick convulsive shudder, and drawing up his hands clutched feebly at the wound. His eyes glared savagely at his foe, and an expression of intense hate and defiance fixed itself upon his dark, bloodless face.

"The Great Spirit is good," said Ka-nee-no at length, with hard, labored breath. "The Apache is dead."

The young warrior was greatly exhausted by the severe struggle he had undergone, and much weakened by loss of blood from the wound made by the knife of the Apache. Removing his hunting shirt, he found a great gash in his side from which the blood freely flowed. Forcing together the severed sides of the wound as well as he was able, he drew the wide belt of his pouch tightly about it, and replacing his hunting shirt, fastened his knife belt firmly outside. Then dragging himself slowly forward, he once more approached the brink of the mesa and looked down in the cañon and the forest beyond.

Not a living being could be seen. A faint moaning sound awakened by the breeze in the forest fell upon his ear. Almost imperceptible at first, it grew stronger as he listened until it filled the deep cañon beneath him with a great, unearthly wail.

It was the funeral dirge of the evil spirits for the Apache he had slain.

The young warrior drew back in terror from the brink, aud at once hastened to escape. Stopping for a moment in his flight to tear away the scalp of the Apache, he hurried forward again with the ghastly trophy fastened to his girdle. Quickly mounting his horse he threw himself forward on the animal's neck and rode furiously away across the mesa to join his companions.

"Me-ra!" cried To-mé, in a tone of surprise, as the young warrior sprang from his horse and sank exhausted upon the ground. "Ka-nee-no has blood on his blanket."

"And a fresh scalp at his girdle," said O-see-to excitedly. "Has Ka-nee-no no words in his mouth?" asked To-mé, hurriedly.

"Yea; Ka-nee-no has words in his mouth," said the young man, speaking slowly, and with much labored breath, "and they will make the hearts of his brothers rejoice. The Apaches are hid in the forest, down in the cañon. Ka-nee-no knows not how many. One came up the trail to the top of the mesa, to watch for the coming of the people from the council. Ka-nee-no wounded him sore with an arrow, but the Apache was brave and bore his wound like a warrior. He was stronger than Ka-nee-no, and his knife was ready and sharp. It cut deep and Ka-nee-no is weak, because his blood has run out.

"The Great Spirit is good, and the scalp of the Apache hangs as a trophy at the girdle of Ka-nee-no.

"When the Apache was dead, Ka-nee-no once more looked down in the cañon, and into the great forest beyond. The Apaches could not be seen, and Ka-nee-no's heart was made glad. They had not heard the twang of his bow string, nor the death cry of their comrade. But while Ka-nee-no looked down, a great wailing cry came up from the cañon and made him afraid. Ka-nee-no has spoken. There are no more words in his mouth."

"Ka-nee-no has done well," said To-mé, with great animation. "The squaws will sing praise in his ears when he goes back to his lodge, and the hearts of the warriors will be glad when Ka-nee-no shall call them his brothers. The squaws will sing of his trophies, and his wounds, and the young men will gather at the door of his lodge. Ground corn and sweet milk, and fresh meat and salt will wait for the coming of Ka-nee-no in every ho-gan in the nation."

The young man, much enfeebled by great loss of blood, and stiff and sore from his wound, raised himself up with difficulty on his elbow and gazed intently at the speaker. His eyes burned with an unnatural brightness as he listened to the glowing words of his leader, and his frame trembled with delight that he could not suppress.

He had performed a brave deed and his companions had hastened to speak words of praise, and do him great honor. His thoughts wandered quickly to his home, and his fancy pictured the glorious reception awaiting him there upon his return. He could already hear the voices of the women, and the shouts of the men. He could see the chief of his clan, pressing forward through the throng, to bid him welcome and speak words of praise. He could see the eyes of the young warriors fixed upon his trophies, glad to do him honor, but envious of his fame. His blood coursed quickly through his veins, as his mind dwelt upon the picture his fancy had created, and raising himself, unconsciously, he sat upright and assumed a proud, haughty air. Thus would he bear himself before his people, in the glorious hour of his triumph. Not a quiver of a muscle, nor a motion of his frame should reveal the workings of his heart. Silently and proudly would he ride, indifferent and responsive to the praises of the crowd.

"Hist!" cried To-mé, as he caught sight of the animated face of the young man. "Ka-nee-no must cease to talk to himself. He must lie down and sleep, that he may grow strong again."

"Yea," said Ka-nee-no, abstractedly. "The words of To-mé are all good."

He raised his head mechanically as he spake, and instantly a sharp twang of pain awakened him rudely from his reverie and dispelled the bright vision that had covered his wounds with forgetfulness. To-mé hastened at once to his assistance, and laid him down gently on the ground.

"To-mé is kind," said the wounded warrior thankfully, "and his words are all good."

He moved about restlessly for awhile, and then, closing his eyes, fell into a light, troubled sleep. Sometime after midnight he suddenly awoke to full consciousness again. His companions stood silently about him, holding their horses and ready to mount. Raising him gently to his feet they lifted him carefully upon his horse, and then springing quickly into their saddles, followed their leader out on the mesa.

Turning immediately to the West they rode slowly forward, keeping as close along the edge of the forest as the low overhanging limbs of the stunted trees would permit. Occasionally they halted for a short time in the deep shadow of some great tree that towered above its fellows, to listen

and to permit their wounded companion to rest. At length,
after a long distance had been accomplished, they suddenly
changed their direction and cautiously approached the brow
of the mesa, searching the ground as they proceeded to find
a trail leading down into the cañon.

The watchful and vigilant Apaches, schooled in all the
devices of the war-path, had doubtless placed sentinels to
watch all the trails near their encampment. It was necessary, therefore, to get some distance away before an attempt
to descend into the cañon should be made.

A narrow, indistinct trail was finally discovered leading
down the steep face of the wall, and the party at once dismounted and began the descent. The trail was scarcely
practicable for the animals, and a long time was consumed
in getting them down. When the descent was accomplished
at last the party at once mounted again, and turning to the
East rode slowly toward the place where the valiant Ka-nee-
no had seen the enemy in the forest.

Within the half of a mile from the spring near which the
Apaches were now doubtless concealed, the peon herders had
built a strong corral of timber and stones for the temporary
protection of their flocks from the storms and the attacks of
wild beasts. To reach this corral if possible, without the
knowledge of the enemy, was now almost a necessary precaution. Halting, therefore, while some distance away, the
young leader sent forward a single warrior on foot, to discover whether it would be prudent to proceed. The warrior
soon returned with a favorable report, and the party again
moved cautiously forward, halting repeatedly as it went and
using every possible precaution to prevent the Apaches from
discovering its presence. These efforts were at last entirely
successful, and the warriors, dismounting from their horses,
led them one after the other through a narrow opening within the enclosure.

XII.

The last day of the great festival had come, and the gathering crowds awaited with impatience the beginning of the final contests for wagers and honors.

Races were to be run over again, and feats of strength and of skill were to be repeated to satisfy the demands of champions who had been defeated in former trials.

Successful gamblers smilingly awaited the rich harvest that experience had taught them to expect during the wild excitement of the day. Poor dupes who had still something left, longed for the beginning of the games, with the hope that they might win some of the rich wagers which they knew would be hazarded by reckless players like themselves.

Buyers and sellers who had failed to agree upon the value of horses and weapons, and of maidens and sheep, waited anxiously for each other, to receive hoped for concessions, or to make new propositions.

Expectation was on tiptoe, and the excited people hurried rapidly from one place to another, anxious lest some wonder should occur which they might fail to witness.

The woman Po-lone stood near her camp fire gazing intently at the crowds. She had promised the medicine man to break up her encampment when the sun shone into the the top of the lodges, and follow him to his ho-gan. But a few hours yet remained to make the necessary preparations for her departure; and speak her adieus to her friends from the north. Suddenly the temptation came strong upon her to slight the promise she had made and spread her robes on the ground for another test of fortune with her cards. It would be a sacrifice to her passion for gambling, which she had not thought of before, if she should now tear herself away at the very hour that gave her greatest promise. The medicine man might be angry, but she could appease him with a gift, and plead the importunities of her friends to excuse her unintentional delay.

She turned about to select some trinkets from her store to wager at the opening of the game. While she was thus engaged and lingering over her ornaments, undecided which to take or to leave, she suddenly caught sight of the tall, graceful form of the young chief approaching her encampment. As he drew near she suspended her work and hastened to spread a robe on the ground for his use.

Without uttering a word, the chief sat down on the robe, and drawing his pouch before him, proceeded with great deliberation to take from it some pulverized tobacco, and to roll a small portion within a piece of fine husk which had been cut from the inner covering of an ear of Indian corn. When he had completed his task, he raised his eyes languidly and gazed for a moment at the woman who had seated herself near him, and then at the smoldering embers of her fire not far away. Comprehending his wishes the woman arose quickly to her feet and hastened to bring him a partially burned stick upon which living coals yet remained. Her guest received the services with a grunt of approval, and after lighting his tobacco, returned the stick with a similar expression, to indicate that he was thankful and pleased.

He puffed away vigorously at his improvised cigar, and the smoke curled in a great cloud about his face. He sat silently the meantime, gazing vacantly upon the ground. At last, when the tobacco was consumed, he turned hastily to the woman and nodded his head familiarly towards her as though he had just observed her for the first time since his arrival.

"Po-lone breaks up her encampment to-day and rides to the south?" he said enquiringly.

"Yea," answered the woman quickly, wondering how the chief had discovered that such had been her intention, and hastening with her answer lest her latter purpose also might somehow or other have been discovered. "Yea, Po-lone rides when the sun shines in the top of the lodges."

"Po-lone is wise," said the chief, "and knows which is best."

A long silence followed the conventional remark of the chief during which both he and the woman sat gazing vacantly at the ground. Po-lone busied herself the meanwhile with her thoughts, wondering how the young chief had learned of her promise to break up her encampment at mid-day, and the chief sat patiently waiting for the woman to speak concerning the purpose for which he had come.

At last the woman raised up her head and turned her eyes in the direction of her guest as though she intended to speak. The chief glanced languidly towards her, and gravely inclined his head to listen to her words. She hesitated for a moment as though in doubt what to say, and then cast her eyes in confusion upon the ground. It was a question of doubtful propriety she desired to ask, and one which the chief would hesitate probably to answer, unless it was put with ingenious adroitness. She had therefore carefully chosen the words she deemed it best to employ, and had selected others to hang about them and conceal them from conspicuous view, like leaves that partially obscure the branches upon which they grow.

In blissful ignorance of her ultimate purpose, she hoped that the chief might be drawn on unconsciously by this means to tell her how he had learned of her intention to break up her encampment. But at the last moment some

defect in the meaning of the words she had chosen suddenly
became apparent, and she remained silent. When the chief
found that the woman had no words in her mouth, he
dropped his head and again cast his eyes on the ground.   '

Another long silence ensued, each waiting for the other to
speak, with the hope that some word might be spoken that
would spare a useless committal. Often individuals sat
thus, side by side, hour after hour, waiting patiently and
silently, one upon the other, for some word of encouragement that promised success for some favor sought, some
trade desired, or the acceptance of an offer for a maiden.

To the proud and haughty warrior, or the still more proud
and haughty chief, the mortification of a refusal was always
felt most intensely. No more complete humiliation could be
experienced by these lords of creation, than that which
followed a refusal. They sat in silence, therefore, at the
lodges of their friends, to whom some offer or request had
been previously made, waiting with patience until they were
assured of success.

The visit of a warrior for such purpose was usually anticipated by his friend. The offer that had preceeded his
coming, had not been made with a view of an immediate
acceptance, for that might involve sometimes a refusal,
but for consideration at some future time. When he came,
therefore, and sat silently at the lodge or within the encampment, it was presumed that he had come for his answer.
When he received the encouragement he expected, the bargain
might proceed at once, thereafter, to its conclusion, but
when his host remained persistently silent, the warrior
could wrap his blanket about him and take his departure,
thankful that no word had been spoken which could be used
to fix the actual purpose of his visit.

Nah-nee-ta stood at a distance, watching the chief and
her mother, as they sat silently in their places. Their ex-

pressionless faces gave her no indication of the intention of either. She had heard the chief make his offer of horses, but neither she nor her mother had expected his visit before their return to the village. The dwarf had told her of the offer which To-mé had made, and she had anxiously awaited his coming, hoping constantly that he would be the first to sit in her mother's encampment, to await her words of encouragement. Her heart sank within her as she observed that the chief sat silently waiting for his answer. She knew her mother too well to indulge in the hope that her preference for To-mé, which she had endeavored to make known by artful words in his praise, and never-ending questions that always ended with a sigh, why he came no more to visit at their fire, would be considered or even remembered. She choked back her sobs and restrained her tears as well as she was able, lest she should be observed, and attempted like a dutiful daughter to reconcile herself in the best way she could to what now appeared to be inevitable.

It would be worse than folly, she attempted to reason with herself, that she should make her life miserable in a useless struggle against fate.

From her infancy she had been taught that it was immodest and improper for a maiden to look with favor upon a warrior. Had it been known that she had permitted herself to indulge in a choice, public opinion would have denounced her as a wanton, and unworthy the confidence of a husband. She sat down quickly and wiped away the tears she had not been able to suppress, wondering why it was that her thoughts would continue so constantly perverse.

Po-lone was busied the meanwhile in preparing her questions, and some time had elapsed before it occurred to her mind that the chief had come for his answer to the offer he had made for her daughter.

"Me-ra," she said, hastening to speak, lest her delay might be regarded as intentional. "The heart of Po-lone is made glad, because the chief has now come. She has kept his words in her heart, and they are all very good."

The chief nodded his head, and grunted in reply.

"How many horses did the chief offer?" she asked, hesitatingly.

"Two," he replied, and after a pause he added decidedly, "Mariano offered two, and no more."

"The chief is rich," said the woman, "and there is no other maiden like Nah-nee-ta in all the nation."

"Two horses," he replied stubbornly.

"The chief is rich," urged the woman, "and a horse is not missed from his herd. The heart of Po-lone will be sad if Nah-nee-ta goes from her lodge for the common price of a maiden."

"The words of the woman are wise," he said at length. "A squaw that is fit for a chief, should be worthy of more than the common price of a maiden. Po-lone shall choose three of the best horses from the herd of the chief, if she will. But the ears of Mariano are many," he added quickly, "and he will wait now no longer for his answer."

"The words of the chief are all good," she said submissively. "When Po-lone returns to the South, she will select the horses from the herd of the chief, and he shall take the maiden to his lodge."

And so it was done. The girl was sold. The beautiful Nah-nee-ta had gone for a price, like a slave or a horse, to a new master.

The mother smiled upon the chief, and the chief nodded his head and grunted his approval. Then drawing his blanket about him, he rose to his feet and strode haughtily away towards his encampment, without uttering a word.

It may be that such things occur all over the world, and that traffic in lives and affections is common. It may be that the power of wealth and position is used everywhere to enslave the fair and helpless. If such is the case, a difference exists only in method, as people are rude or refined. The savage, untaught and uncouth, acts with simple direction, and scorns to conceal the purpose in view. The civilized man, enlightened and courteous with labored finesse and tortuous ways, employs the silent power his possessions may give. The methods are all that can differ. The end is virtually the same.

As soon as the chief was well out of sight, Po-lone summoned the dwarf, and bade him hasten to the pasture and drive in the horses. He gazed at the woman for a moment in utter surprise, and then turning about pointed with his finger towards the animals, still tethered securely at the line where they had remained since the previous day.

"Po-lone has lost a piece of her head," he said at length, turning his perplexed face towards her, while he kept his finger extended in the direction of the horses.

"Yea," she said hesitatingly, "Che-no speaks true. Po-lone has lost a piece of her head."

She gazed stupidly about her while she spake, apparently endeavoring to recall why the animals had been kept at the line, when they should have gone to the grazing grounds some hours before.

"The woman bade Che-no make ready to ride," said the dwarf.

The words of the peon brought quickly to her mind her original purpose to break up her encampment at midday, and ride to the ho-gan of the medicine man.

"Yes," she said quickly, "Che-no speaks true. His ears hold the words that he hears. He may go to the herd and make ready to ride."

As the dwarf turned away, a broad smile crept slowly over the heavy face of the woman, and she chuckled aloud and rubbed her hands vigorously together.

"Me-ra!" she murmured. "The thoughts of Po-lone were fast in her head. The horses stood tied at the line in view of the chief, and Po-lone has troubled her head because of his words."

"Bah!" she exclaimed, as she suddenly remembered that her purpose to delay her departure had been defeated by her hasty reply to the question of the chief. "Po-lone is a child. She shut her eyes when she turned her face to her herd, and carried her head in a bag."

It was impossible now to delay her departure, and bidding her daughter go with her, she set out at once to find her friends from the North and bid them adieu. When she had completed this duty, she returned to her encampment, and mounting her horse rode quietly away across the great plain, followed by her daughter, her peon and her herd. Turning about as she rode slowly along, she looked back wistfully at the busy scenes she was leaving behind. Then shaking her head sorrowfully she murmured again, "Po-lone was a child. She carried her head in a bag."

The sun had already disappeared behind the great mountain range on the west of the plain, when she overtook the disorderly herds of the medicine man. From some cause or other it had been delayed in its journey, and was now winding about in the broken foot hills, at the base of the mountain.

The woman reined in her horse and followed on leisurely behind it. The great rugged face of the mountain before her was flooded with the last rays of the sun, and ablaze with the glitter of imbedded stones that reflected the light. As she gazed indifferently at the glorious vision, her wandering eyes rested at last upon some diminutive objects away to the south, moving slowly upward near the top of the mountain.

Her curiosity was awakened at once to know what they were, and she watched them attentively until they had passed out of view. Once again as she looked she caught sight of the objects upon the top of a great spur of the mountain that jutted far out on the plain. Their forms were clearly defined against the bright sky, revealing the figures of horses and men. In a moment they again disappeared from her view, and she saw them no more.

They were doubtless a body of warriors, but where they were from, or who they might be, she could only conjecture.

Some expedition of her people perhaps, endeavoring to conceal its departure, or even it was possible, a daring band of their enemies, out on some present mischief.

Counseling with her fears, she grew anxious and alarmed, and at last hastened forward to report what she had seen to the medicine man.

"There are warriors on the mountain far away to the south," she whispered hurriedly, as she rode to his side.

"The eyes of the woman are sharp," he replied. "The warriors she saw are her friends from the clans of the head chief Barbon-ce-to." Then after a pause he continued. "They ride to the south to look at the tracks that frightened the peons, in the pasture grounds of Me-su-la."

She waited awhile and rode on at his side with the hope that he would give her at length some further information concerning their mission. She waited in vain. He had told her all that he deemed it proper she should know, and rode on thereafter in silence, ignoring her presence. She drew away from him at last, and halted by the side of the trail for the coming of her herd.

The ascent of the mountain had now been fairly begun,
and the unruly animals soon became quiet enough as they
toiled along one after the other, up the difficult path.   The
storm of the previous night had nearly obliterated the trail,
and in places had worn great furrows across it, or covered it
from sight with great piles of stones or with masses of earth
The darkness coming on, rapidly increased the difficulties
of the ascent, and rendered the progress of the herds still
more labored and slow.   Long delays now often became
necessary to permit the animals and the people to rest, or to
await the removal of obstructions from the trail.   At last a
peon ignited a torch of resinous wood and preceded his
master to light up the way.   Guided by the torch the caravan advanced more rapidly than before, halting repeatedly,
however, and moving on spasmodically again as the animals
found strength to proceed.   At last the top of the mountain
was reached, and a long delay was then made to permit the
horses and people to take needed rest before the journey was
resumed.

Under the guidance of To-mé the medicine man had ridden from his ho-gan to the encampment at the mouth of
the cañon in nearly the same time that it had taken him
now to effect the ascent of the mountain.   It was comparatively easy, however, to make the descent, and owing to the
presence of the warrior, the servants had followed in order
and silence.

The feeble old man had lost control of his peons and
squaws, and they had spent the whole of the day in wrangling and quarreling about their several duties in following
the herd.   Their progress had therefore been delayed, and
the darkness had overtaken them at last, before the journey
had fairly begun.

The most difficult part of the route, however, had now
been successfully accomplished, and a well-traveled trail,

that could easily be followed, extended before them. They moved on again, after a time, and at last reached the end of their journey at a late hour in the night.

On the following morning the woman arose early from her robes and waited impatiently at the door of the lodge for the appearance of the medicine man. He had been greatly fatigued by his journey, and his sleep was unbroken until late in the day. He got up at last and came out of his lodge and directed some food to be brought. When he had eaten, he turned to the woman who stood waiting near by, and quietly asked:

"Did the Great Spirit whisper words in the ears of Po-lone while she slept?"

"Nay," she answered. "Po-lone heard no words while she slept."

"Let the woman ask all the people," he said. "The omens are good, but Me-su-la knows not that the Great Spirit is near."

She hastened away and questioned the squaws if either had dreamed in the night. They smiled at her earnestness, and shook their heads in reply. She searched then for the peons, but they had all gone with the herds to the pastures, and no one could tell where they could be found. Poor Che-no sat near to the ground and hung down his head in despair, because he was the last to be questioned.

"Did Che-no hear words while he slept?" she asked him at length.

"Yea, Che-no heard words," he replied with great earnestness. "They fell in his ears while he slept."

"Come, quick!" she exclaimed, and seizing the astonished dwarf by the arm, she raised him to his feet and hurried him along towards the ho-gan.

"The peon heard words while he slept," she exclaimed, as she pushed him before her into the lodge.

"And what were the words the peon has heard?" asked the medicine man gravely, without raising his head.

Poor Che-no could find no words to reply. He gazed anxiously about him, and trembled with fear. But the terrible things he had expected to see in the lodge of the medicine man had all gone away, and gathering courage at last, he replied:

"Che-no walked in the snow while he slept, and his feet were numb with cold."

The medicine man kept his eyes on the ground for a time apparently absorbed in his thoughts. At last he raised his head slowly, and gazing fixedly at the dwarf, said sharply,

"The peon may go."

Poor Che-no, more frightened than ever, sprang through the door of the lodge and hastened away.

"The peon has but half of a head," said the woman, looking out of the door at the retreating form of the dwarf.

"Yea," said Me-su-la, "the woman must wait for some better words to show that the Great Spirit is near."

"Nay, nay," she replied, "the peon speaks true. He has but one tongue in his head, and his words have never been wrong."

"Then Me-su-la will go to the mountain," he said, "and when the Great Spirit has spoken, he will come back to his ho-gan again."

When the woman came out of the lodge a squaw led a horse to the door, and assisted her master to mount, and then followed after him on foot, as he rode slowly away up the side of the mountain.

He came back at last looking wearied and sad, and entering his lodge lay down on his robes.

"The woman may go to the door," said the squaw, "to hear the words that Me-su-la has brought from the mountain."

Po-lone hastened at once to the lodge and stood in the door, impatient to hear the words he had brought.

"The woman has come for her answer," he said as he raised himself up on his robes. "Me-su-la can speak, but he knows not that the Great Spirit is near. The words in his mouth may be bad." Then after a pause he continued. "The girl may go to the chief. Me-su-la has spoken. The woman may go."

Po-lone turned slowly away, ill satisfied with the words she had heard. The object she sought had been gained, but the pleasure she hoped for was obscured by her fears. She had sold the girl to the chief, confidently believing that by the gift of a horse, she would be able to influence the use of the most powerful means in her favor, and would secure a full approval of her course. The means had doubtless been used, but they had signally failed to secure the strong assurance she had desired. She had been taught from her youth to rely upon these means for counsel and guidance, in all the affairs of her life. The Great Spirit, she believed, would visit with terrible disaster those who asked for his guidance, if they failed to obey. Strong as was her desire to accomplish her purpose, her faith and her fears would have compelled her to submit to the result of her final appeal. But what that result had been, she could only conjecture. The manner as well as the words of the medicine man had awakened her fears. Once before he had spoken, but his words then were strong. He had spoken again, but his words now were weak. At first he said, the girl must go to To-mé, but now, she might go to the chief. At first or at last, the medicine was bad, and evil lay in one or the other.

She reached her encampment at length, and directed the dwarf to make ready to ride. When all was prepared, she mounted her horse and rode slowly away, following the trail

to the South.   Absorbed in her thoughts she rode quietly
on, without uttering a word, or looking about her.   Nah-
nee-ta rode close by her side, awaiting with patience some
sign that might foreshadow her fate, and Che-no, the dwarf,
followed listlessly after, more asleep than awake.   The
animals moved slowly along, almost as they pleased, and
cropped at the grass as they went.

Several miles were accomplished in this tedious way, and
the caravan slowly approached the great forest that bordered
the valley on the East.   It had scarcely arrived at the edge
of the wood, when two Apache warriors sprang suddenly
out from the cover of bushes that grew near the trail, and
yelling like demons and waving their blankets, ran quickly
into the midst of the herd.   The horses took fright in an
instant, and reared back on their haunches in terror, and
then plunged madly about to escape.

At the first appearance of the Apaches the woman gave
up in despair.   Aroused suddenly from her gloomy medita-
tions. she saw the evil she dreaded already upon her.   Para-
lized completely and bewildered by fear, she made no attempt to control her frightened horse, or to effect her escape.
Recovering directly her presence of mind, she seized on the
mane of the horse and held fast for awhile.   The terrified
animal, frantic with fear, plunged madly about and threw
her at last to the ground.   Springing at once to her feet she
ran quickly among the bushes at the side of the trail, and
under their cover escaped to the forest above.   Concealed
by the trees, she climbed up the side of the mountain until
at last she was safe from pursuit.

In the meantime Nah-nee-ta held fast to her horse and
was carried far out in the valley.   Then gathering the reins
in her hands she obtained some control of the animal, and
bid fair for awhile to escape.   But just as her hopes were

beginning to dawn, the creature sprang suddenly aside and threw her with violence to the ground.

So soon as the Apaches had accomplished their immediate purpose and frightened the animals beyond all control, they hastened to capture the dwarf. One arrow after another in rapid succession whizzed past his head, and at last one struck in the side of his horse. The poor frightened beast struggled forward as though it would fall, but recovering again it ran quickly away down the valley and into the wood. It appeared soon again in the open, but its rider had escaped and was gone.

Nah-nee-ta was bruised by her fall, and unable at first to rise from the ground. She struggled at last to her feet and hastened to escape to the woods. The Apaches perceiving her purpose, ran quickly in pursuit and soon overtook her and compelled her to stop.

One of her captors then remained near her to prevent her escape, and the other, with lasso in hand, hurried after the horses. The animals had partially recovered from their fright and were wandering slowly about in the valley. Quietly approaching the horse that appeared least alarmed at his presence, he cast his rope dexterously over its head. Springing at once upon its back he rode after the others and attempted to drive them before him.

In the meantime some peons attracted by the noise left their herds in the mountain and rode into view far above in the valley. The quick eye of the savage caught sight of the peons as they emerged from the forest, and fearing they were warriors on their way back to their homes from the council, he abandoned his purpose and rode quickly away to join his companion. The two held a hurried consultation and decided upon immediate flight. Taking the captive up behind him, the mounted Apache galloped away down the valley, closely followed by his companion on foot.

XIII.

Poor Che-no was first to come down from the mountain when the Apaches were gone. Slowly emerging from the cover of the forest, he fell on his knees and crawled stealthily out to the thicket that grew near the trail.

Noiselessly parting the bushes before him, he pushed out his head and gazed down the valley in the direction the Apaches had fled. They had gone out of sight, and the valley lay quiet and peaceful before him. The horses had gathered together and were leisurely moving about cropping the grass as they went.

The peon drew out of the bushes at last and slowly raised himself up on his feet. He stood undecided for a while and then as his courage increased moved farther out in the valley, halting again and again as he went, and gazing furtively back at the bushes to see that his way of escape was preserved.

Approaching the herd, he succeeded in catching a horse, and springing at once on its back, gave way to his joy in a shout. The Apaches may come again if they choose, for Che-no, no longer asleep, had now the control of means of escape. His shout was soon answered by a cry from the mountain, and shortly thereafter the woman appeared, cautiously emerging from the forest.

The dwarf had been completely absorbed in his efforts to accomplish his own personal safety, and had quite entirely forgotten the terrible calamity that had befallen his mistress. The appearance of the woman recalled to his mind the dreadful disaster, and quickly converted his joy into grief. He bowed down his head with remorse that he had proven so useless in the time of her need, and rode slowly forward to meet her.

"The Apaches came quick," he said, with emotion, while he averted his face, "and Che-no did all that he could."

"Yea," said the woman, "Che-no did well. Let him go to the herd and bring a horse for Po-lone."

The dwarf hastened away much pleased at the kind words of his mistress, but greatly surprised at the calmness she displayed. Her eyes burned with an unnatural brightness, and traces of weeping remained, but her manner gave no indication of the anguish and rage she suppressed. The peon soon returned with the horse she was accustomed to ride, and when she had mounted he followed her out in the valley again. He kept his face constantly turned to the south in the direction the Apaches had fled, while the woman slowly looked over the herd and deliberately counted the horses to see how many were gone.

"It is strange," she exclaimed when she had finished the count, "but two of the horses are gone."

"One of the horses lies dead in the edge of the woods," said the dwarf. "He was shot in the side with an arrow."

"The Apaches are cowards and dogs," murmured the woman, "and something has scared them away."

"Eh!" exclaimed the dwarf, catching part of her words, and glancing uneasily around as he spoke. "The Apaches? Where are they?"

"Hist!" cried the woman. "What comes from the north?"

The dwarf turned quickly about and gazed up the valley. One view was enough to confirm his worst fears. Four mounted men were in sight, galloping rapidly towards them.

"Apaches!" he shouted, and digging his heels in the side of his horse, and lashing him hard with the end of a rope,

he forced the animal over the valley at the top of its speed.
As he drew near the bushes under which he had found concealment before, he reined in his horse and sprang from its
back, and secreted himself quickly again. He held fast in
his hand one end of a long lariat, attached to the neck of
the horse, and carried it with him to the place where he hid.
Recovering at length somewhat from his fears, he pushed
out his head and gazed wildly about. To his utter amazement,
a horse stood bridled and saddled before him, held fast by
a rope in his hand. Some moments elapsed before his poor
wits could recall that the horse was his own. He remembered
at last, and bounding out quickly from his place of concealment, sprang once more on its back and again darted headlong over the valley. This time he rode straight for the
forest, and directly disappeared under cover of the trees.
He halted at last, and turning quickly about peered anxiously out in the valley.

Perplexed beyond measure he could scarcely believe what
he saw. Some evil agency he feared had enchanted his eyes,
and caused him to see what could not possibly occur. He
moved nearer to the edge of the wood where the view was
less interrupted, and looked out again. The same doubtful
vision once more met his gaze, but with greater distinctness
than before. The four mounted men from whom he had
fled, had arrived at the spot where he had abandoned his
mistress, and were peaceably gathered about her. They
were certainly not the dreaded Apaches, if the vision was
true, but rather some friends of the woman who had come
to help. But his fears had enthralled him, and he looked
doubtingly on, expecting each moment some direful change
to occur in the scene. In the meantime his horse grew impatient to return to the herd, and moved forward whenever
his master gave way on the rein. Little by little the horse

moved along, gaining a few steps at a time, until in the end he carried his master well out of the wood.

When the dwarf came into view from the valley, the woman rode forward a short distance towards him and shouted his name and beckoned him on with her hand. At the sound of her voice his fears were somewhat allayed, and after a brief hesitation he rode over the valley to meet her. As he drew near where she sat on her horse, he gazed for awhile at the strangers, and then hung down his head with mortification and shame. They were peons from the village of Me-su-la, and herders of horses and sheep. They had heard the shouts of the Apaches, while they tended their flocks in the mountains, and fearing that some disaster had happened to a herd of their master, had hastened below to discover the cause.

"The chief Mariano rides with his warriors from the encampments to-day," said the woman, addressing herself to the peons, "and a runner could meet him in the great valley below, and tell him the words he has heard from Po-lone."

The peons remained silent while the woman looked anxiously in each of their faces. At last she turned slowly around and looked at the dwarf. He was deficient in courage she knew, but possibly, she thought, his fears would induce him when once well away, to ride for his life to reach the side of the chief.

"The Apaches have gone to the South," she continued, "and the trail to the great valley below goes straight with the sun."

"Che-no is tired," he said plaintively, "and if he should ride, Po-lone would be alone with the herd."

The woman bowed down her head in despair.

"Yea, yea," she murmured, "the warriors speak true. The peons are cowards, and fit only to watch while the horses eat grass."

"Has the woman a horse for the runner to ride?" asked one of the peons. "Me-su-la might be angry if a horse from his herds should be taken."

"Yea," she replied, "the peon may take the best horse in the herd of Po-lone, and keep him as a gift when his journey is done."

"Then Pablo will ride," said the peon. "Will the woman remain where she is?"

"Nay," she replied, "Po-lone will follow the trail down the valley, and ride for her lodge. The night will soon overtake her, and the darkness will hide her from the Apaches."

The peon at once rode away to the herd and carefully looked at the horses. He found one at last that suited his purpose, and casting a lasso over its head, led it out from the herd. Placing his saddle and bridle upon it, he sprang on its back, and waving his hand to his comrades, rode rapidly away to the West, and soon passed out of view in the forest. So soon as he was gone his companions bade the woman adieu, and hastened to return to their flocks in the mountain.

The sun had already sunk low in the West when the woman resumed her sad journey. Poor Che-no was nervous and fearful, and gave her but little assistance in driving the herd. The darkness at last gathered heavily about her and rendered her progress more difficult than before. But she still pressed forward undismayed and determined, and eventually arrived safely at her lodge.

In the meantime the Apaches hastened on with their captive to join their companions, whom they expected to find somewhere concealed in the cañon. They soon changed their direction in following the course of the valley, and passed out of view from the point where the attack had been made. Halting here for a while they secreted themselves in the forest, and watched up the valley for the approach of the horsemen who had frightened them away. They plainly observed them as they galloped to the spot where the woman awaited their coming. They could see her as she moved slowly about, pointing with her finger to the South, as though directing the pursuit. They waited with increasing anxiety, expecting each moment to see it begin. It was important to know how many pursued, and the manner in which they would start. They waited on, therefore, until they grew tired with their long fruitless watching.

"They are cowards," said one of the Apaches, "and afraid to pursue."

"Yea," replied the other. "They are cowards and peons as well. They have come from the flocks in the mountain. My brother has fled from the herders of sheep."

"They are not far away," said his companion suggestively. "My brother can quickly return where they are."

"Nay, nay," he replied. "A warrior never fights with a peon. Let them stay where they are, and talk with the woman."

The Apaches, no longer apprehensive of pursuit, drew leisurely out of the wood, and slowly moved on down the valley again. Falling soon in the trail over which To-mé and his warriors had ridden a short time before, they followed it on until late in the night, riding and walking alternately, as one or the other grew tired. They halted at last about midnight, and talked for awhile in low tones with each other concerning the course they should take for the cañon.

"The trail goes slowly away to the East," said one of the Apaches, "and the cañon lays more to the West."

"Yea," said the other. "The trail leads to the village where the warriors have gone who rode down it to-day."

At last they decided to abandon the trail and cross over the mountain on the East of the valley. It was well for them indeed that they adopted this course. A mile or two further beyond, the valiant To-mé and his warriors lay close by the path with vigilant sentinels around them. The heavy tramps of the horse on the hard beaten trail, would have speedily betrayed the Apaches and cost them their lives.

Turning abruptly away from the path, they moved over the valley and directly began the ascent of the mountain. Climbing slowly along from one difficult point to another, they gradually accomplished the ascent to the summit. From this great elevation they could plainly distinguish the course of the cañon by a dark narrow line extending some distance to the right and left, not far from the foot of the mountain. Changing their course now more to the South, they immediately began the descent.

Great masses of rock of irregular shape lay dispersed all about them upon the face of the mountain. Some evil agency that existed within had forced them out thus, through the earth, from the heart of the mountain. They were broken and cracked and full of great fissures, where things that were evil made their abode.

The Apaches moved quickly along, winding tortuously about in their efforts to avoid these places of danger. They halted at length, and made their captive dismount from the horse. Then fastening the ends of a buckskin lariat to the saddle they bound the other tightly about her. When this was accomplished, the warriors both mounted the horse and once more continued their journey.

The Apaches were frightened, and had hastened to take refuge on the back of the horse, where they had been taught to believe the power to harm them would be seldom employed.

The captive followed after in silence well pleased with the change, and hopeful that now she might make her escape. She attempted at last to untie the hard knots of the rope with which she was bound. She had scarcely begun when she was jerked to the ground, and dragged roughly along for awhile, before she could recover her feet.

"Hist!" cried one of her captors in a voice full of anger, and seizing again on the rope as he spake, he jerked her once more to the ground. She struggled again to her feet and walked quietly on as though she had abandoned all hope of escape. She feigned well her submission, and after a time was less rigidly watched than before. Stooping quickly to the ground, as she hurried along, she gathered a small stone in her hand. Stooping quickly again she picked up another without being seen. Then drawing a loop of the rope under the folds of her blanket, she attempted to wear it in two between the stones in her hand.

In the meantime the Apaches had arrived at the base of the mountain, and were nearing the edge of the mesa. As they moved quickly on they caught a glimpse, now and then, through the thick undergrowth, of the great open region beyond. They halted abruptly at last, on the edge of the plain, appalled by the danger before them. Great masses of rock, in fantastic disorder, had suddenly presented themselves in their way. To the right and the left, the thick undergrowth presented a change of direction. Before them a single opening in the midst of the rocks, presented the only means of escape.

They ventured at length, and lashing the horse almost to a run, dashed into the opening. The ground trembled beneath the feet of the horse and gave back a hollow response to the tread of its feet. It had nearly got through when it suddenly sunk to its knees in the earth. The terrified animal sprang forward with a desperate plunge and barely escaped going down with a great mass of earth, that had sunk into some cavernous depth underneath.

As the Apaches came near to the opening between the great rocks Nah-nee-ta perceived that the time to attempt her escape had arrived. Unobserved by her captors she drew out the loop of the rope she had carried concealed in the folds of her blanket, and attempted to break it. But the few strands that remained unabraided were unusually strong, and resisted her utmost endeavor.

While she continued her efforts to sever the rope she was drawn rapidly forward into the opening. Rendered desperate now by her failure to effect her release, she threw herself backward and pulled on the rope with all of her strength. She was jerked instantly forward with tremendous force and barely succeeded in keeping her feet.

On the way down the mountain she had repeatedly attempted to unloosen the hard knots of the rope under the cover her blanket afforded. She now nervously tried these again. They were harder and firmer than ever, and a few brief trials convinced her that her efforts were useless. In utter despair she dropped her hands by her side, and submissively followed her captors.

She ran rapidly forward with her eyes on the ground, selecting her steps as well as she could, scarcely able the meanwhile to keep on her feet. A quick muffled cry from one of the Apaches at length attracted her attention, and raising her head she perceived that the horse was sinking down in the earth; an instant thereafter she was drawn suddenly forward with terrible force, and fell helpless and stunned in the midst of the treacherous place, and sunk out of sight in the ground.

The Apaches glanced back as they emerged from the pass to see what became of their captive.

The lasso was broken and the captive was gone. The evil thing from the cavern had seized her and carried her away to its home in the heart of the mountain.

They halted at last, and dismounting from the horse came cautiously back near the rocks and pleadingly called her,

"Muchacha! muchacha!"

They called her again "Muchacha! muchacha!" and begged her to speak, if by any good fortune their voices could reach her. A bare hope still remained in their minds that the lasso had broken before the evil thing had opened the ground, and that she might have escaped to the bushes. They pleaded and threatened by turn as a change of their humor occurred, and waited and listened in vain. No response was received, except the faint echo of their own doleful voices returned from the cavernous rocks.

"Hist!" cried one of the Apaches, "something comes over the mesa."

Then falling instantly down on his face he placed his ear near the ground, intently. He raised up his head in a moment and gazed to the East.

"There is tramping of horses," he said, "not far away on the mesa."

Again placing his ear to the ground he listened an instant, and then sprang to his feet.

"The tramping comes nearer," he said, in alarm. "Bring the horse quick to the bushes."

And leading the way he hastened to the west, along the edge of the mesa. Halting at last at some distance from the pass, he assisted his companion to force the horse in the bushes and covered its head with a blanket to prevent it from neighing. Then, crouching down by its side, they awaited the approach of the horses. They had scarcely effected their concealment when a Navajo warrior rode out of the dark-

ness and passed slowly along a short distance before them.
At the first sight of the Navajo one of the Apaches eagerly
fixed a barbed arrow to the string of his bow, and drew it
back quickly to shoot. But his companion restrained him,
and pointing to the east said softly,

"More horses are coming, and the arrow of my brother
would bring quick pursuit." Then he added somewhat angrily
"Would it please him to hide in the holes on the side of the
mountain ?"

The Navajo horseman passed slowly on and had nearly
gone out of sight when he suddenly reined in his horse, and
turning around sat silently waiting and watching about him·
In the meantime several horsemen followed quietly on and
passed near the place where the Aapaches lay hid in the
bushes. When they reached their companion they halted,
and after a brief consultation, started on slowly again.
Changing their course now abruptly to the left, they rode
out over the mesa towards the great cañon, and were soon
lost to view in the darkness.

When they had passed out of sight, the Apaches turned to
each other and conversed in low tones for awhile. It was
evident to them from what they had seen, that the Navajo
warriors were now on their way to the cañon to search for
their brother Apaches, and surprise them if possible under
cover of the darkness. The party that had passed them was
doubtless a small portion only of the force that was gathering to make the attack. The danger that threatened was
great, and prompt action could not be delayed. Their
brothers were doubtless well guarded by vigilant sentinels,
and could not possibly, they believed, be completely surprised; yet some lives might be saved, or even a victory assured by a warning in time.

But their duty seemed first, they agreed, to follow their
enemies and endeavor if possible to discover without any

doubt, what their purpose might be. Springing at once to their feet, they led the horse from the bushes and mounting again, started out in pursuit. Riding cautiously forward, they soon came within hearing of the tramping of feet, and then slowly moved on keeping well out of sight. As they came near to the brow of the mesa, one of the Apaches dismounted and went forward on foot. Falling frequently down on the ground as he proceeded, he endeavored to get under the darkness, peering anxiously the meanwhile before him. He came back at length and hurriedly approached his companion.

"They have gone down a hard rocky trail," he said, quickly, "and the feet of the horses made a great noise as they went."

"It will be easy to follow," replied his companion, moving on with the horse as he spoke.

"Nay, wait," cried the other, as he seized the horse by the bridle. "The Navajos, too, will hear tramping of feet, if my brother leads his horse down the trail."

"They will escape," pleaded the rider, impatiently, "if my brother delays."

"Nay," said the other, "get down from the horse and turn him loose on the mesa. The pursuit must be silent, and my brother must walk."

Without further remonstrance the Apache dismounted and hastened to hobble the horse. Drawing its fore feet together, he fastened them firmly with a small piece of rope, and removing the bridle turned the horse loose on the mesa. Thus fettered, the animal was securely confined, and would scarcely be able to get far away before its masters could return to find it again.

The horse turned quickly aside when it found it was free, and with short labored steps tried hard to escape. Growing weary at last with its almost fruitless exertion, it suddenly stopped and began to nibble a dry tuft of grass that the wind had carried out on the mesa. When the Apaches perceived that the horse had ceased all its efforts to make its escape, and stood quietly feeding, as though it was familiar with such cruel bondage, they turned to each other and nodded heads to express themselves pleased.

"He made little trouble," said one of the Apaches. "He has been hobbled before."

Without further delay they now hastened forward and soon reached the brow of the mesa. Halting here for a moment, they gazed cautiously over into the dark cañon below and listened the meanwhile intently. Not a sound could be heard, nor a moving thing seen, to reward their precaution. The elder Apache then placed himself in advance, and falling at once on the ground, crawled slowly along down the trail. His companion reluctantly followed his example, and crawled on impatiently behind him.

"My brother goes slow," he whispered at length. "Why should he walk on his knees?"

"Hist!" cried the other, stopping quickly and turning about. "Can my brother see the trail in the cañon?"

"Nay," he replied, "the cañon is dark. Not a thing can be seen."

"Let him speak then again," said the elder quite sharply, "when he knows that no danger is hid where he is not able to see. The trail comes from the darkness," he continued more kindly, "and winds up the great wall to the light of the sky. Sharp eyes may be watching. How many, who knows? Let my brother keep close on the ground, or he must go on alone."

"The words of the warrior are good," said the other in a tone that betrayed his impatience. "Let him go on as he pleases. His brother will follow and walk on his knees."

They gazed at each other a moment in silence, and then slowly resumed their laborious journey. A long time was consumed in descending the trail, before the great darkness was reached. Then raising themselves by degrees to their feet, they moved on again with bodies half bent and soft noiseless feet, until at last they arrived at the end of the trail in the cañon. They halted for awhile when they found themselves down, and listened for some indication to guide them. But the moaning of the wind in the trees, on the side of the mountain beyond, drowned every other sound, if any there was, before it could reach them. They moved on directly again, and groping their way in the darkness, discovered at length a well defined path that followed the course of the cañon.

Turning at once to the east they followed the path for awhile, stooping down often as they went slowly along to feel with their hands for the tracks of the horses. At times they succeeded in finding a track, but the loose earth had partially filled the impression and rendered it hard to determine which way the animals that made it had gone, or whether indeed the track was a new one or old. One of the Apaches at length sat down on the ground and covered himself with his blanket. Then taking a little hard stone from his pouch, he struck it repeatedly with the back of his knife until a spark fell at last on a small piece of tinder he had placed to receive it. The resinous touch-wood ignited at once, and burned slowly without making a blaze. The Apache leaned forward and held the coal near the ground, and blew it almost to a flame with his breath. It gave a pale, feeble light, but revealed to his gaze with sufficient distinctness the shape of the track. Quickly pushing the tinder into the ground to extinguish the fire, he threw his blanket aside and sprang to his feet.

"They have gone to the east," he said quickly, "and are not far away. The sand is still falling down in the track."

Starting forward once more, they followed the trail to the East, feeling their way with their feet. At times as they hurried along they stumbled outside of the path, but always regained it again after brief search had been made. They continued on thus for a long, weary time, and were beginning to fear that their efforts to overtake the Navajos would be useless. They halted at last, and stooping down on the trail, attempted once more to feel with their hands for the tracks of the horses. To their utter surprise, not a track could be found They stood for a moment undecided and perplexed, and then turned about to search back on the trail. They had scarcely begun, when their attention was suddenly attracted by a slight noise in the rocks some distance away to the right of the trail. They stopped instantly and listened for awhile with the hope that the noise would be repeated again. But the deep, constant moaning of the wind in the trees filled their ears to the exclusion of all other sounds. They whispered together for a moment, and then cautiously made their way towards the spot from which the noise had been heard. They had ascended some distance from the bottom of the cañon, and had partially got out of the dense darkness, when they came suddenly in view of the Navajo warriors, where they sat quietly waiting for the return of a scout who had been sent on before.

The Navajos moved on directly, closely followed by the skulking Apaches, and took refuge at last in a high-walled corral built for the protection of sheep. When this was accomplished the Apaches perceived that the Navajos were now in position to make the attack, when the time they had chosen should come. Stepping quickly away, they returned to the trail in the cañon, and moved hurriedly on to alarm their companions.

XIV

The chief Mariano walked proudly away from the woman's encampment well pleased with the exchange he had made.

The beautiful girl he had bought would bring joy to his lodge with her smiles. She would reign like a queen in the ho-gan of the chief, and the squaws and the peons should serve her like slaves.

He was delighted and happy, and his joy was at last made complete when he remembered that his rival, the runner To-mé, with all his good looks and agreeable ways, had been unable to compete in the end for the prize, with so illustrious a warrior as himself.

As he approached his encampment, he was met by a runner with a message from the head chief Barbon-ce-to, who awaited his coming at the mouth of the cañon. He hurried forward at once and soon reached the place which the runner had named. As he came near he was hailed by the watchman who stood at the entrance, and directed to proceed to the great council chamber, whither the head chief Barbon-ce-te had gone.

As he passed into the entrance, a number of warriors who had hurriedly gathered attempted to follow.

"Nay, nay," cried the watchman, springing down in the narrow passage before them. "The chiefs only can enter. Barbon-ce-to has spoken."

The warriors drew back and stood in a group near the entrance, indignant that the great common right to visit the chamber when the chiefs were assembled, had now been denied them. They conversed with each other in low, angry tones, and recited their grievance in forcible words to those who were gathering about them. They grew more rebellious

as the number of their hearers increased, and at last had
well nigh succeeded in inducing the crowd to force its way
to the chamber to demand that the rights of the people
should at once be restored.   At this critical juncture an old
warrior of venerable appearance separated himself from the
crowd, and climbing to the top of a rock, held out his hands
to express his desire to speak.   The people at once became
quiet, and drew near the rock to hear what the old warrior
would say.

"Me-ra?" he shouted, at length.   "Is the nation too
great for my brothers?   Have they joined with the Apaches
and the Utes to destroy it?"

When he had spoken these words, the old man bowed
his head on his breast and paused for awhile, that the people
might have time to reflect on the full meaning and force of
the words he had used.   Then raising his head he continued
his speech.

"My brothers," he said, "the old warriors of the nation
are wise.   They know all the customs, and are glad when
they see them obeyed.   When they speak all the people
must listen.

"Me-ra, my brothers," he continued, with great animation.   "When a new chief of a clan has been made, all the
chiefs meet together in the great council chamber.   It has
always been thus in the nation.   What harm has been done?
Has not the nation grown stronger, because the chiefs are
at peace with each other?   Who ever before has spoken hard
words because the chiefs were alone?

"Me-nar-rah has spoken.   Is there a warrior before him
who can say that his words are not good?"

The old man stood in his place for awhile, and gazed
down on the crowd as though he challenged reply.   But the
people were silent, and no spokesman appeared to champion

their cause. He came down at last from the rocks, and walked slowly away from the crowd. As soon as he had gone the warriors began to disperse, and when he halted some distance away to look back at the crowd, they had all disappeared. Not one of the loud talking braves had remained to assert that his rights had been lost, and to demand that they should be restored.

"They are fools," said the old man, disdainfully. "They are mad when unable to do as they please, and madder than ever when nothing prevents. They deserve to be peons and watch the sheep with the squaws."

He walked on again in a moment, busying himself as he went, with thoughts of the men and the times of his youth.

"Ah me," he exclaimed with a sigh. "The people and customs grow bad. When Me-nar-rah was young they were good. The warriors were braver and stronger than now. The chiefs were the bravest and strongest of all. One chief in those days," he continued, "could have scattered the cowards that talked of their rights at the mouth of the cañon, like the wind scatters the leaves. Ah me, what a change. Me-nar-rah is glad he is old."

He cast his eyes on the ground and shook his head sadly like one in distress. But his humor soon changed when he joined with the crowd, and witnessed some tests of endurance and skill. He clapped his hands loudly, and assured those about him who were willing to hear, that such wonderful things had never been accomplished before.

In the meantime Mariano passed on to the great council chamber, where he found all the chiefs of the clans already assembled in council. When he entered, the head chief arose from his seat and bade him welcome once more to his place in the chamber. Mariano stepped forward to take his seat in the circle, when the deep, solemn voice of the head chief bade him stop where he stood.

"The chiefs have a question to ask of my brother," he said, gravely. "Let him answer in peace. Can he keep his own secrets? Can he forever conceal the words which a brother has spoken?"

The young chief was much grieved that such questions should be asked him, and he slowly replied in a tone very formal and bitter.

"Yea, Mariano is a chief and a warrior. His tongue is not loose like a squaw's."

"Yet again," said his questioner, "Mariano must answer. The eyes of the chiefs are upon him. Could the water, or fire draw words from his mouth, that a brother had spoken in secret?"

"Nay, nay," he replied, with much indignation. "The head chief alone can ask such a question. Mariano is weary, his ears burn with shame."

"Once more," persisted the chief. "Once more must he answer. Could the spirits of evil, or the torture of knife or of arrow, draw words from the mouth of Mariano, which a brother had spoken in secret?"

"Nay," he replied, fiercely. "Why should Mariano be asked such questions as these? Is there a chief in the nation who doubts him? Let him speak if there is."

"It is well," said the head chief, impressively, addressing himself to the chiefs. "The answers which Mariano has made are all good. Do my brothers agree that the secret may safely be given?"

The chiefs nodded their heads and grunted their assent.

"Mariano, my brother," Barbon-ce-to continued, "the chiefs have a secret. It has been kept since the nation began. To divulge it is death; to keep it is strength. My brother will listen."

Then calling before him three chiefs of the clans, he briefly addressed them.

"My brothers," he said, "the head chief will make known the great secret to the chief Mariano. He is worthy and true. But should he forget, and reveal the great secret, what then?"

"Thy brothers will kill him," they cried with feigned fierceness. "Yea, kill him at once, like a dog."

"It is well," said the chief. "But if my brothers should fail."

"Then," they replied, "all the horses and the flocks of thy brothers shall belong to the head chief of the nation."

"And then?" asked the speaker, looking enquiringly, as he spoke, at the circle of chiefs.

"And then," they replied, springing at once to their feet, "the head chief shall lead, until the secret is safely returned to the chiefs."

"Yea, yea," said the chief, "Barbon-ce-to will lead. The secret must never be lost, or the nation will die. The head chief alone may disclose it, in the great council chamber. None other than a chief can hear it and live."

"If the great secret were known to the people," he continued, "the winds would soon bear it far away to the north, and the Utes, and the men with white faces would come. It would ride on the storms to the west and the east and the Mexicans would come. The young men of the nation would be wasted in war. Let my brothers keep the great secret that the nation may live."

When Barbon-ce-to had finished, the chiefs all returned to their seats, and Mariano was left standing alone.

"My brother has listened to the words of the chiefs," Barbon-ce-to continued, "and he can speak now at last for himself. Will he hear the great secret, and keep it forever?"

"Yea," he replied, "Mariano will hear the great secret and keep it forever."

"It is well," said the chief, and motioning Mariano with his hand, to a seat with the chiefs, he continued. "My brother; near the top of the wall in the cañon Bo-neet, an opening can be seen in the rock. It is broken and rough and as large as a lodge. The wall hangs out above it, and no mortal can reach it from above or below. This opening goes into the wall, and under the mesa, to the foot of the mountain beyond. There it comes out to the top of the ground, and is covered with sticks and with earth to conceal it.

"My brother," continued the chief, lowering his voice almost to a whisper. "In this opening great masses of silver are found. Three chiefs must always go together. While one has gone into the cavern the others must watch."

The chief paused for a moment and then added quickly.

"The council is ended. The chiefs will return with their clans to their lodges when the sun shines again in the east. Barbon-ce-to has spoken."

The chiefs remained for some time in the chamber after the council was ended, and conversed with each other concerning the affairs of their clans. They retired at length, one ofter the other, and slowly dispersed to their several encampments. A great portion of the day had already been spent when the chiefs eame together in the chamber, and when they now slowly emerged from the mouth of the cañon the shadow of the mountain that lay on the west, had fallen again on the plain.

The darkness soon gathered, and at length put an end to the contests and games, and closed the last festival. The people reluctantly dispersed when the great fair was ended, and made their way slowly to their several encampments. For a time they moved restlessly about from one place to another, gazing hurriedly as they went at the groups that

were forming around the camp-fires. Here and there individuals found friends whom they sought, or heard subjects
discussed that induced them to stop and sit down in the
groups. They all found their places at length, and for a
while talked together with great animation of the contests
and games of the day. But as the night wore away, their
voices died down almost to mere murmurs and finally ceased
altogether. One after the other, they stole quietly away
from the groups, and retired at last to their blankets and
robes.

A bright, beautiful morning succeeded, and the peons and
squaws made haste to be ready for an early departure. But
the indolent warriors remained in their robes as long as they
could, and grumbled and scolded when they were eventually compelled by the noise to arise. They wandered about
then from one clan to another, making final arrangements
for the forays and journeys they had planned. The day was
half gone before they had bidden adieu to their friends and
were ready to ride. The war chief, Manu-le-to, was the
first to break up his encampment, and depart with his clan.
Then, one after the other, the chiefs rode away with their
people to the north and the east, until the last clan had
gone.

Mariano had already dispatched his peons and squaws
with the herds and had mounted his horse to depart, when
the head chief, Barbon-ce-to, came riding towards him.
Taking Mariano aside he briefly informed him of the departure of To-mé with his warriors, for the pasture grounds of
Me-su-la.

"It was useless," he said, "that the runner should go,
but Me-su-la was urgent and full of fear for his herds."

Then again bidding Mariano adieu, he rode hastily away
and followed after his clan.

Mariano sat still for a moment after Barbon-ce-to had gone, looking out on the plain where the encampments had been. The place that so lately had been covered with wild, thronging people, was already deserted and silent. He turned his horse quickly about and rode rapidly away to the south, following after his people, already some distance away.

The report of the peons was highly improbable, and gave him but little concern. The most vigilant warriors of his clan had remained in the south, while he had ridden to the council, and every pass in the mountains and every trail in the valleys, had doubtless been examined each day during his absence, by these trained men of war. That the peons should be the first to discover the presence of an enemy was simply absurd. But it annoyed him excessively to think how persistently fate threw the runner To-mé in his way. It could scarcely be possible that his rivalry now would be other than harmless. But the thoughtless and hot-headed ways of the runner might lead him to commit some desperate excess, and he heartily wished him success in finding the enemy he sought. He found consolation at length in the thought that he soon would be able to take the girl to his lodge and thus end forever this persistent annoyance.

He caught up directly with the herds, and riding on past them, placed himself in advance of his warriors, and pushed on ahead as rapidly as possible, with the purpose of making his camp for the night in the cañon Bo-neet. But the darkness overtook him at length, several miles yet away from the cañon, and compelled him to stop. He reined in his horse and sat waiting with his warriors, until the herds should arrive. The clatter of the feet of a horse, galloping rapidly over the plain from the mountain on the east, suddenly attracted his attention, and almost immediately after a mounted peon rode out of the darkness towards him, and hurriedly asked for the chief Mariano.

"The peon speaks now to Mariano," said the chief. "Let him speak on."

"Pablo has come from the woman Po-lone," said the peon, "with a message for the chief Mariano."

"That To-mé, the runner, is searching for tracks in the pastures, by the side of the woman," said the chief, with great indignation.

"Pablo is a peon," he replied with some hesitation, "and guards the flocks of Me-su-la. He knows not the runner To-mé, nor the place where he rides. The woman was alone with her herd."

"Yea, yea," said the chief, with increasing impatience, "and sent the peon to speak the evil words of his master, that the girl should not come to the lodge of Mariano."

"Pablo knows not," said the peon, in doubt of the meaning of the words of the chief. "The woman has gone on alone, and the Apaches have fled with the girl to the south."

"The Apaches!" cried the chief, in surprise. "Let the peon speak quickly all the words which the woman has sent."

"Two Apaches sprang out from the bushes on the side of the trail," said the peon, "and frightened the herd of the woman with their yells and their blankets. The horses ran madly about and the woman and her peon fell off and escaped to the mountain. But the girl, Nah-nee-ta, fell hard from her horse on the ground and could not escape. Four peons of Me-su-la, who were watching their flocks in the mountain not far away, heard the great noise and hurried down in the valley. As they came near, the Apaches ran away with their captive. One rode on a horse from the herd of the woman, and the other ran after on foot. The woman bade Pablo speak all of these words to the chief."

When the peon had finished, Mariano turned quickly about, and calling several warriors by name, bade them hasten to join him, prepared for a long and determined pursuit. Then calling before him one of the principal men, he placed him in charge of the people and herd and bade him move near the base of the mountain and camp for the night.

In a short time the warriors whom the chief had selected gathered hurriedly about him, prepared for the pursuit of the Apaches. Then placing the peon in front to pilot the way, they set out without a moment's delay. They moved forward rapidly, sometimes urging their horses almost to a run, and soon reached the place where the attack had been made on the woman.

The services of the peon being now no longer required, he was permitted to return to his flocks in the mountain. As soon as he was gone, Mariano spread out his warriors like skirmishers in line, and moved down the valley. Those who were most skillful in searching for trails, dismounted from their horses and preceded their comrades on foot. They moved rapidly about here and there, searching on the ground as well as they could in the darkness, for foot-marks of horses or men. But all of their efforts proved useless. Not the least trace of the signs which they sought could be found. Even the foot-marks which the Apaches had made, when they left the great trail to cross over the mountain, escaped them. Passing on down the valley they came out at length on the mesa.

"Hist!" cried a warrior, almost in a whisper, "a fresh trail of horses goes away to the west," and falling down on his knees as he spoke, he crawled slowly along on the ground, carefully examining the trail he had found. His comrades on foot, gathered hastily about him, and stood waiting to hear his decision. He sprang up at last on his feet and quickly exclaimed : "A war party trail ! The horses go straight in one path."

As soon as he had spoken, his comrades sprang quickly away, and with their ;bodies half bent and their heads near the ground, followed rapidly along 6n the trail. Sometimes two or three, more eager than the others, ran far ahead and searched on the ground for the path, to enable more rapid pursuit.

Mariano rode after, well pleased with the eagerness his warriors displayed, and almost surprised at the rapid progress they made. He was now well assured that the trail had been made by his enemies, and he pushed on with the hope that he would be able to overtake them before the night wore away. The two Apaches who had captured the girl had doubtless gone out from this party to watch for the coming of the people from the council, and to steal horses from the herds of Me-su-la. They had already returned to their companions, he thought, and he would find the poor captive at last, bound and helpless, in the midst of their camp.

The hours passed rapidly away, and the day dawned at length on the warriors, still pushing forward in eager pursuit. As the first rays of the sun fell across the great plain, they arrived at the brow of the mesa. Halting here for awhile they gazed cautiously down in the dark cañon below. The wind for a' moment had died entirely away, and its fitful moaning in the forest had ceased. The great cañon lay below them, but faintly revealed to their view, and as silent and lifeless as the grave.

The chief had been greatly encouraged at first when the light had revealed the foot-marks which the Apaches had

made in the trail. Their peculiarly shaped moccasins had
left an impression in the dust that plainly disclosed who
they were. They had doubtless, he thought, bound the girl
on the horse, and had driven the animal before them. But
the foot-marks of the Apaches had scarcely been found
when a horse was discovered hobbled out on the mesa. A
warrior soon caught it and led it up to the chief.

"The horse belongs to the herd of the woman," said the
warrior, "and the Apaches who rode it are not far away.
Its back is yet wet with the sweat."

"The girl must have gone before them on foot," said the
chief, and springing down from his horse, he himself
searched along on the trail for her tracks. Several warriors
at once joined with the chief, and continued the search for
some time. At last they discovered the place where the
Apaches had dismounted from the horse, and carefully examined the ground. But the tracks of the captive could
nowhere be found.

"They have killed her," said the chief, in despair. "Or
it may be," he added in a more hopeful tone, "that she has
made her escape. Nay, nay," he continued, after a brief
pause. "It could scarcely be so. They have killed her,
the cowards! The Apaches are dogs!"

He stood quietly thinking for a moment and then harshly
exclaimed : "Let the warriors make haste now to follow the
trail."

They moved on at once and soon began the descent into
the cañon. The rough, narrow trail wound tortuously
about on the face of the great rocky wall, scarcely wide
enough often for the passage of a single horse at a time.
The difficult descent caused frequent delays, and when the
last warrior in the long crooked line reached the bottom, the
light had fallen down in the cañon and revealed clearly to
view the foot-prints of both horses and men in the sand.

The chief now moved forward at the head of his warriors, and led the way down the canon. He had not ridden far when he reined in his horse and bending far over looked intently for a moment at the moccasin tracks on the trail.

"Me-ra!" cried a warrior who had ridden to his side. "The dogs stopped here in the night to examine the trail."

Springing down from his horse, the warrior looked carefully around where the Apaches had sat in the path. Then, pointing at length with his finger on the ground, to a diminutive bed of white ashes, he said, quickly :

"The dogs struck a light. See the ashes of the tinder they used."

As he spoke he leaned forward and brushed the ashes away with his hand. As he did so, he exposed a portion of. the tinder, half buried in the sand, and yet unconsumed. He raised it up carefully and blew the ashes away with his breath.

"Me-ra!" he cried. "The tinder yet burns. The dogs are not far away."

"Hist!" cried the chief. "Let the warriors make ready. The Apaches are not far away."

He hastily drew an arrow from his quiver and fixed it on the string of his bow. Then, shaking his hunting knife loose in its sheath, that it might easily be withdrawn, he moved on again down the cañon.

He had gone on for some time, expecting each moment to see the Apaches spring out from their concealment near the trail, to offer him battle or make an attempt to escape, when he was suddenly startled by the sound of a horse galloping rapidly towards him. Almost immediately after, a beautiful white horse came into view, rushing madly up the cañon, with an arrow sticking fast in its side. The warriors looked on in amazement. There was not a white horse in all the herds of the nation, and where this one had come from they could not even conjecture. If by any improbable chance it had escaped from the herd of the Apaches, how came the barbed arrow in its side ? A few warriors rode hastily out from the trail to intercept it, but the chief peremptorily ordered them back to their places. The horse ran on beyond them, and then wheeling about, came once more towards them and forced its way among the horses in the line, as if attempting to free itself from the torturing weapon in its side. A warrior at length reached out his hand, and, withdrawing the arrow, held it up quickly with a loud anxious cry.

"A Navajo arrow!" he exclaimed. "Our brothers fight somewhere with the dogs."

"Move on !" cried the chief. "Let the led horses go."

Almost instantly thereafter the well-known battle cry of the Apaches broke the great silence, and awakened the lazy echoes that slumbered along the great wall of the cañon.

The cry of the Apaches was answered directly, from the same place it seemed, by a cry much feebler in volume, but bold and defiant. Then the lazy echoes responded with the wild battle cry of the nation.

"To-mé the runner !" cried a warrior with delight. "He yells like a panther. There is hot work for the dogs where To-mé the runner makes battle."

The chief lashed his horse to a run, and the warriors, at once breaking from the line, rushed down the cañon pell-mell beside him.

Brave To-mé had been sorely beset. He had gone out from the corral in the early gray of the morning, leaving the wounded Ka-nee-no in charge of the horses, and had sought to surprise the Apaches in their camp. He had found them awake and awaiting his coming. They had largely out-numbered his little command, and had well nigh surrounded him before he had discovered his danger. The darkness alone had saved him from total destruction, and enabled his escape. Fighting his way back to the corral, with the wounded O-see-to in his arms, he had held his assailants at bay until now. With terrific yells they had gathered at last about the enclosure, and had already begun a desperate assault. Within a brief time the brave To-mé and his comrades would doubtless have perished in the unequal encounter.

At this critical moment the chief and his warriors swept down the cañon, and with the wild battle cry that had often struck terror to the hearts of their foes, dashed headlong in the midst of the Apaches. Joining at once in the cry, To-mé and his comrades sprang out from the corral and rushed into the thickest of the fight.

The battle that followed was most sharply contested, but brief. The impetuous charge of the chief and his warriors could not be withstood, and the surviving Apaches, abandoning their herd and their wounded, fled away for their lives, and hid from their pursuers in the forest and among the rocks on the side of the mountain.

The chief at length stopped the pursuit for the time, and returned with his warriors to the cañon.

"The fears of the dogs made them fleet," said the chief, "and the young men are weary."

To-mé's little band had suffered severely. Himself and one other alone had escaped with their lives or from wounds. O-see-to had been twice sorely wounded, and poor Ka-nee-no lay dead in the rocks. Several warriors of the chief had been wounded or slain, and the bodies of a number of Apaches lay scattered about here and there on the ground.

The chief and his warriors at once went to work to bind up the wounds of their comrades, and render such other

assistance as they were able to give. While thus engaged,
the people whom the chief had left behind in the valley
where the peon had found him, came into view, moving
cautiously along down the trail through the cañon. When
they caught sight of their friends they hurried forward and
gathered hastily about them. The chief then surrendered
the care of the wounded and dead into the hands of his
people, and calling To-mé to his side, said kindly,

"Mariano rides now to the south in pursuit of the dogs.
Will To-mé ride with him?"

"Yea," said the runner, "To-mé will be glad to ride on
the trail with the chief."

"The heart of Mariano is made glad," he replied, "by
the words of To-mé. Let him make ready to ride for many
days on the trail."

A short time was consumed by the chief in selecting more
warriors to increase the strength of his command, and to
take the places of those who had been wounded or slain.
Then blankets and food were obtained, and the quivers re-
plenished anew. When all of these things were accomplished,
the chief hastened away with his warriors and soon disappeared in the forest.

XV.

While the chief was engaged in selecting more warriors, to increase the strength of his command and supply the places of those who had been wounded or slain, he called to his side an old warrior in whose fidelity and good judgment he trusted, and directed him to proceed with all possible haste, so soon as he was gone, to make search for the girl. The chief spoke to the old warrior in a low indistinct tone, that those about him might not hear what he said.

"She may be dead," said the chief, "or she may have escaped to the mountains, and wanders helpless and bewildered in search of her people. Find her trail," continued the chief earnestly, "and hasten to overtake her or find where she died. If Mal-tush-malo comes back to his lodge with good words in his mouth, he shall choose the best horse in the herd of Mariano for his own."

"Mal-tush-malo has heard the words of Mariano," replied the old warrior, turning his expressionless face to the chief, "and they will all be obeyed."

Mariano had deemed it his duty to accompany his warriors in pursuit of the Apaches. He would gladly have sent them under some competent leader and remained the meantime behind to search for the girl. But the place of a chief when his country was invaded, was at the head of his warriors, and the custom of his people left him no other course to pursue. He might possibly have violated the custom in this instance without blame, since the flight of the Apaches had virtually ended the invasion, but such a course was involved in some doubt, which the chief thought it best to avoid. For the first time in his life, he prepared for the war path with reluctance.

The presence of the runner To-mé served further to perplex him. The runner belonged to the clan of the head chief, Barbon-ce-to, and his movements could not well be controlled. If he remained, he would soon learn of the fate that had befallen the girl, and would doubtless set out in hot haste, and find her at length if she was still alive. Should the chief invite him to ride with the warriors in pursuit of the Apaches, he would be compelled to entrust him at times with important commands, which might bring him new honors and greater renown.

The chief hated the runner intensely, and held him a rival for the honors of war and the homage of the people. And, greater than all, he yet held him a rival for the possession of the girl, inspired by the hope that she would eventually be found. He selected at last what appeared at the time the less evil of the two, and hastened to invite him to ride in pursuit of the Apaches.

As soon as the chief and his followers had gone, preparations were made to remove the wounded and dead. Several wide blankets were joined strongly together at their edges, from one end to the other, with sinews and thongs. Through each of these sacks two long poles were thrust, to be used by the bearers as handles. A robe was then thrown upon each of the litters, and a wounded warrior placed gently upon it, between the two poles. Those of the wounded who were able to ride, were tenderly placed upon horses selected for the ease of their carriage. The bodies of the dead warriors were rolled up in blankets, and bound carefully upon the backs of such animals as were accustomed to the bearing of burdens.

The body of poor Ka-nee-no was placed in charge of a few mounted warriors to be carried to his friends in the north. So soon as the necessary preparations were made, they moved silently away on their sorrowful journey, and soon passed out of sight up the cañon.

When they had gone the warriors again mounted their horses and moved slowly on down the cañon. They were followed by the wounded who were able to ride, and then by the litters, each borne by four peons or squaws. The other peons and squaws, hushed to silence by the presence of the dead, followed after with the herds.

As the procession neared the village, a runner was sent forward to announce its approach, and to give the names of the wounded and slain.

The village seemed almost deserted when the runner arrived, but the sad news that he brought flew quickly about from one lodge to another, and a great crowd of people soon assembled about him. As he proceeded to announce the names of the dead, the people stood waiting in silence and in anxious suspense to learn who of their number had fallen. One name followed another until the runner at length ceased to speak, as though he was done. A great sigh of relief escaped from the people, and they murmured their thanks to the Great Spirit that none of the young men from the village had been slain. But the runner held up his hand, and the people became silent again.

"One other," he said sadly. "One other is dead. Brave Tish-me-walla of the village was slain."

The runner bowed his head on his breast to express his great grief, and turning slowly about rode away from the crowd. The squaw of the brave Tish-me-walla wrung her hands in despair, and bitterly lamented the cruel fate of her master. She sat down on the ground and swayed herself to and fro, moaning piteously the meanwhile, overcome by her grief. Several squaws gathered around her and attempted in vain to console her with words of praise for her master.

They raised her at last from the ground and bore her away to her lodge.

In the meantime the procession had reached the end of its journey and had halted at the edge of the village. The wounded warriors were then quickly borne away to their lodges, or to those of their friends in the village. The body of the brave Tish-me-walla was removed from the horse that had borne it and carried to the lodge where the squaw had been taken, and laid gently by her side on the ground.

When this was accomplished a few mounted warriors were placed in charge of the other dead bodies to bear them away to their friends. They departed at once to the east and the west to search in the valleys and cañons for the ho-gans of the dead comrades they carried. As soon as they were gone the warriors rode slowly on through the village, and then dispersed to their lodges.

For three days and three nights the poor squaw of the brave Tish-me-walla, mourned the death of her master. She blackened her face with charred sticks from the fire, and threw ashes and dust on her head. Several squaws from the village came to mourn with her, and kept up a dismal wailing and moaning all the day and the night. The favorite horse of the dead warrior was taken to the mountains and killed, that his spirit might serve the spirit of his master on the journey of the dead. The medicine man of the clan came often to the lodge, and with solemn demeanor mumbled meaningless words, and beat on his drum to keep the evil spirits away.

On the third day in the morning the peons and squaws went away to the forest and brought dry bushes and sticks, and green branches of sweet smelling cedar for the funeral pile.

The body was then arranged in the corner of the lodge on a raised bed of blankets and robes, and all the weapons of a warrior were placed at its side. Then the lodge was filled up with the bushes and sticks and the green branches of cedar which the squaws and the peons had brought, and at last, as the sun disappeared in the west, a burning torch was thrust in the midst of the pile.

The mourning all ceased when the torch was applied, and the great crowd of people that had gathered stood silently watching the flame as it grew. It burst out at length from the top of the lodge when the night had come on, and revealed the spectral-like features and forms of the people, in its soft mellow light.

In the early morning, while the fire yet smouldered in the ashes of the funeral pile, the squaw of the dead Tish-me-walla drove her herd from the village, and went her way to the mountains, to build her ho-gan anew in some quiet valley far away from the spot where she had mourned her bereavement.

As the procession moved down the cañon from the place where the battle had been fought, old Mal-tush-malo drew silently aside, and hid himself in the forest by the side of the trail. When the last herd had gone past him and the people were all out of sight, he came from his concealment and at once made his way up the cañon. Hurrying back on the trail over which the chief had just passed, he ascended at last to the mesa and crossed it to the mountain beyond. Here the old warrior soon found the tracks made by the horse which the Apache had ridden, and a short time thereafter he came suddenly upon the mysterious place where the ground had gone down. He stood still for some time and looked down in the place with great amazement and wonder.

For many long years a strange story of the existence of a deep, monster cavern hid under the mesa, had been

whispered all over the nation. The people talked seldom
about it, for somehow or other the impression had grown
that a great evil creature that worked harm to the nation
had made its home in the cave. When they spoke with each
other of the mysterious place, they muffled their voices and
looked restlessly about, lest their words might invoke the
great evil they feared.

The marvelous story of the cavern had often been burdened with still more marvelous accounts of the adventures
of a few daring warriors, who had at one time or another
found their way all alone to its dark and lonesome cham-
bers.

But, unfortunately, a peculiar fatality had pursued these
brave warriors, and they had all speedily perished in one
way or another with their adventures half told.

Once every year many chiefs came together and held a
long talk on the mesa, in the presence of the people. When
the talk was all over, and the question at issue had been
fairly discussed, the chiefs had been accustomed to go away
by themselves for a few days of fasting and much medicine
making, among the rocks at the base of the mountain.

Why this evil place had been chosen for these common
meetings had caused the people to wonder, and at times had
given rise to some strange speculations. But the wise medicine men, always ready to teach what they thought pleased
the chiefs, shook their heads sagely and spoke of the customs which the chiefs must observe. They had always met
here to talk with the people, and to make medicine among
the rocks at the base of the mountain. There was no other
place in all the country of the nation, so easy of access, where
the Great Spirit had shown such wonderful evidence of his
great power and strength. And, at least, if the story was
true that an evil creature made its home beneath the great

mesa, its power to do evil things was for a long time restrained, or entirely destroyed, when the Great Spirit came, to whisper words in the ears of the chiefs.

Mal-tush-malo stood still for some time, gazing down where the earth had fallen in. The place was not large, and not very deep. On the side towards the cañon, a small opening had been exposed, through which a warrior might crawl on his knees. The curiosity of the old man was excited at once, when he made this discovery, and obtaining a long stick from the forest near by, he thrust it down in the opening. To his great surprise and alarm, the dark opening extended as far as he could reach with the stick. Withdrawing it quickly he threw it aside, and hastened at once to destroy all the tracks he could find.

"Mal-tush-malo knows nothing," he murmured, when he had completed his work. "His ears have been closed, and his eyes have been shut. All his tracks have gone out, and no one can say that Mal-tush-malo knows the way to the cavern."

He hastened back then, for some distance on the trail he had come, and brushed out the tracks he had made in approaching the place. Then starting once more anew, he followed the broad trail of the chief for some distance to the east, taking care as he went to walk where his tracks could be seen.

In this evil place, from which the old warrior now fled, poor Nah-nee-ta had fallen. Bewildered by fear and blinded by the dust, she lay motionless awhile, expecting each instant that some greater disaster would befall her. But the moments passed on without further cause for alarm, and recovering at length somewhat from her fears, she raised her head from the ground, and rubbed the dust from her eyes. As she sat thus engaged she was startled by the voices of the

Apaches, and falling down quickly again on the ground, she crawled forward to make her escape in the bushes. She went on for some time, quite surprised that the sunken place was so large, and that the darkness had become so intense. She stopped at last quite abruptly, and raising herself to her feet, attempted to determine the proper course for her flight. Appalled by the black darkness, she stretched out her hands and gazed wildly about. Her eyes fell at last upon a small opening, in the direction from which she had come, through which a faint light could be seen. One glance was enough to convince her that she had unwittingly crawled through this opening, into the great evil cavern beneath the broad mesa. For a moment she gave way to her fears, and threw herself down on the ground in utter despair. Gathering courage at last, she raised herself up, and crawled back to the opening with the utmost haste she could make. Passing through the narrow entrance, she found herself once again at the bottom of the place into which she had fallen. She paused for a moment to listen, before venturing further. Then assured by the silence that the Apaches had gone, she sprang out of the place, and fled for concealment to the bushes that skirted the forest. Continuing her flight without a moment's delay, she made her way blindly through the thick bushes and brambles. Unconscious of the direction in which her flight lay, she hurried forward, with no other purpose but to effect her escape from the dreadful Apaches, and the still more dreadful creature that lived in the cavern.

The sharp thorns on the bushes tore her face and her hands, as she pushed recklessly onward, regardless of paths and clear open places that lay in her way. But at last she grew calmer and moved forward more carefully, avoiding the thick bushes as well as she could in the darkness. Her

way was now tortuous, as she ran here and there, still intent
on escape and regardless of her course. She came out at
last on the mesa and stopped there for a moment ˌfor the
first time in her flight, to consider what next she should do.
It was dangerous, she reasoned, to venture out on the mesa
for the Apaches could then easily overtake her if they came
in pursuit. But she remembered directly that the wild
beasts from the mountains often prowled in the forests at
night and were even less merciful than the cruel Apaches.
Casting her eyes to the heavens, to determine her course by
the stars, she started out boldly across the great mesa.

Some time after daylight she came in sight of the village,
and at last reached the lodge of ˌher ˌmother. Po-lone sat
within engaged in gloomy reflections, when the shadow of
the girl fell across the doorway. Raising her eyes quickly,
she caught sight of Nah-nee-ta, her face torn and bloody,
and her garments in rags. She raised up her hands and
cried, "Nah-nee-ta!" at the top of her voice, and then hastened to bring water to wash the girl's face. Nah-nee-ta
returned the warm greeting of her mother by a ghastly attempt at a smile, and faintly responded, "Po-lone."

That was all.

Then all the affairs of the lodge went on as before, and
as though nothing unusual had happened.

When Nah-nee-ta had taken some food she sat down on a
robe and spoke softly in the ears of her mother.

"Nah-nee-ta has but few words in her mouth," said the
girl. "The Apaches fled quickly when the horsemen
rode down into view, and leaving the trail in the valley,
they went up the mountain in haste. Nah-nee-ta was
placed on the horse and one of the Apaches held it fast with
a rope and drew it before him. At last when the darkness
had come, the horse became frightened at something before

it and breaking loose from the Apache who held it, ran
away down the mountain. Nah-nee-ta 'held on for some
time, but at last she fell off, and crawling quickly away, hid
herself in a hole until the Apaches had 'gone. Then she
came back in the valley and followed the trail to the village.
Nah-nee-ta is glad. Her words are all done.''

"Po-lone too is glad," said the woman, "and the heart
of the chief will be light when he hears that Nah-nee-ta is
safe in her lodge."

"The chief!" cried the girl, with well feigned surprise.

"Yea, the chief," replied her mother, rather sharply.

"Nah-nee-ta will be happy in the lodge of the chief.
The peons will come when she calls, and rich robes and
fine horses are better than coarse blankets, and a herd yet to
grow."

The girl turned away to conceal her quick tears, and hid
her fair face in her hands.

"Hey!" exclaimed a rough voice at the door of the
lodge, "are there no words of welcome for an old warrior in
the ho-gan of Po-lone?"

"Yea," answered the woman, turning quickly towards
the door to see who had spoken.

"The old warrior is welcome. Let him come into the
lodge and sit down on the robe."

"Mal-tush-malo is glad to hear the kind words of the
woman," he replied. "He has walked a long distance, and
his feet have grown weary." Then after a short pause, he
added softly: "The chief sent him [out from the sheep
corral in the cañon to search for the girl in the mountain."

Nah-nee-ta became at once greatly alarmed when she
heard the last words of the warrior, and turning quickly towards him fixed her gaze on his face. Some evil fate, she
believed, would most surely befall her if her tracks had

been found in the dust at the mouth of the cavern, and she waited in anxious suspense to hear what more he would say.

" Mal-tush-malo can bear good words to the chief," he continued. " The heart of Mariano will be glad when he hears that Nah-nee-ta is safe in the lodge of her mother."

" Why came Mal-tush-malo so quickly to the lodge ? " asked the woman.

" Hey ! " exclaimed the old warrior with an air of conceit. " It is easy to follow on the trail of a squaw."

" Yea," said the woman, submissively. " Where did Mal-tush-malo find the trail of the squaw."

" In the dust," he replied gravely, turning his stolid face to the woman, and waiving his hand to the north.

" Where ? " cried Nah-nee-ta, in a voice that betrayed her emotion. " Where did Mal-tush-malo find the trail ? Let the warrior speak quick."

" Hey ! " he replied sharply. " The squaw has no patience. An old warrior thinks much before he finds words to speak."

" Mal-tush-malo can speak when he pleases," said the woman.

" Young squaws have no patience," he continued. "Eh ! Where ? In the north. Mal-tush-malo found her tracks in the dust, on the great trail that goes up the valley to the pasture grounds of Me-su-la."

Nah-nee-ta gazed earnestly in the face of the old warrior, in the vain effort to detect some change of expression, that would reveal something more than the words he had spoken. But his great fleshy face remained as blank and expressionless as vacancy itself, and gave no indication whatever to guide her. She knew very well that his words were not true, for she had not followed the great trail down the valley from the pasture grounds of Me-su-la. She was grateful however, that his words had confirmed in some measure the short, evasive story she had told to her mother.

She cast her great, pleading eyes on the ground, and sat wondering what secret lay concealed behind the cautious words of the old warrior.

"Hey!" he exclaimed at length, in a cold, lifeless way. "The flocks from the village have gone up on the mesa, and the trail of Nah-nee-ta can be followed no more. At one place where she stopped for a while, not a track of her foot could be seen, when Mal-tush-malo turned his face to the east."

The girl raised her head quickly, and gazed again in his face, seeking for some confirmation of the hope which his words had awakened. The old warrior returned her earnest gaze for a moment, and then closed his eyes tightly, and shut his mouth hard.

Nah-nee-ta was perplexed for awhile to understand what he meant, but it occurred to her soon that the old warrior desired to inform her without committing himself, that he had discovered her tracks at the mouth of the cavern, and had kindly destroyed them. There could be no other meaning of the words and the signs of the faithful old man.

Her heart gradually grew lighter as this view became confirmed, and a smile slowly gathered and drove the lines of care from her face. The old warrior seemed pleased, and bowed his head once or twice, as though he talked with himself, and then, raising up from his seat, went slowly away without speaking again.

The days now passed quickly away and the people of the village became anxious at length to hear from the chief. A considerable time had already elapsed since his departure, and his return was now constantly expected. Eager eyes watched the passes in the mountains, that led the way to the south, to catch the first glimpse of the runner, which the chief would dispatch to announce his approach.

But the days passed away, one after the other, without bringing the tidings they expected, and the people grew weary with watching. They gathered in groups about their lodge fires, when the night had come on, and shook their heads gravely while they talked with each other. Some dreadful disaster, they feared, had befallen the venturesome chief, and the Apaches, emboldened by success, might appear any moment in sight of the village.

The principal warrior of the clan deemed it prudent at last to send a runner to the head chief Barbon-ce-to, to inform him of the long absence of the chief Mariano, and the great alarm of his people. But before the runner had gone a messenger from the chief galloped into the village in the gray of the morning, and set all the people at once in commotion by his whoops and his yells. They gathered hastily about him to hear the words he had brought. It was evident from the manner of the messenger, that he bore them good tidings, and the people pressed closely about him, in their anxiety to hear every word he would say.

"The chief rides to the village before the sun sets to-day," said the messenger. "He followed the Apaches a long way to their lodges, and drives back a great herd of horses. He has captives and robes, and great buttons of silver from the lodges of the dogs. Scalps hang at his girdle, how many, who knows? The chief led the battle with To-mé at his side. The warriors are all safe, but many are wounded, and the chief must ride slow."

The messenger paused for a moment, and then continued again with a list of the names of the wounded. When he had finished at last, he turned from the crowd and rode quickly away to his ho-gin in the village.

As soon as he had gone the people dispersed and ran to their lodges to spread the good news, and to hasten preparations for dances and feasts in honor of the arrival of the chief and his warriors.

Many peons and squaws were dispatched to the forest as soon as it was light, to bring to the village dry bushes and sticks, and green branches of cedar, to be burned in the night while the dances went on. Others hastened to make ready for the great feast to be given when the chief and his warriors should arrive, and ground corn to make bread, and slaughtered the finest kids that could be found in the flocks.

While these preparations went on the lazy lords of the lodges busied themselves with their personal adornment. They painted their swarthy faces and put on their best garments and girded themselves with white belts of doeskin, adorned with great silver buttons and bright-colored stones.

At last all was ready. Nothing more could be done. There was fuel in abundance placed convenient for the fire, and a great feast prepared that would feed all the clan. The warriors lounged about in their gorgeous attire, and all waited for the coming of the chief.

XVI

The day was well gone when the chief and his warriors came into sight of the village. As they drew near it, a small party of braves, with the chief at their head, rode forward to make the accustomed triumphal display. With loud whoops and yells, they dashed through the village, making the semblance of an attack as they went. Rushing hither and thither, from one lodge to another, they feigned to shoot at the people, or to strike at those within reach, with their tomahawks or knives. The people in turn feigned the part of Apaches, and fled here and there, with loud cries of distress.

"The Navajos! The Navajos!" they shouted. "The terrible warriors from the north have come down. It is useless to fight them. Flee! flee! to the mountains, and hide in the forest."

The warriors halted at length, some distance beyond the last lodge of the village, and turning about returned slowly in solemn procession, to display the choice trophies they had taken in battle. As the chief rode along, he took his belt from his person and waved it slowly before him, to exhibit the fresh, gory scalps with which it was adorned.

Several warriors followed after, quite near to the chief, as the place of the next greatest honor, and waved their belts proudly, to display the ghastly scalps they had taken. Then followed others less fortunate than their comrades, bearing only bright-colored blankets and heavy, rich robes, and great massive buttons of silver. The procession passed on through the village, and then the warriors immediately galloped back to their comrades, whom they had left with the herds and the wounded.

The whole party now once more approached, and the
people *en masse* turned out of the village, and rushed forward to meet it. The wounded warriors were at once borne
away by their friends, and carried tenderly to their lodges,
and mounted peons sent out from the village, drove the
captured herd to the pastures. The warriors of the party
thus relieved from all care, dispersed quickly to their lodges
or to those of their friends.

But a short time elapsed after the arrival of the chief and
his warriors, when the feasting began. Every lodge door
was open, and food was served to all comers, as long as they
remained. But the choicest viands were preserved for the
brave warriors, who had followed on the trail of the Apaches,
and who were now slowly eating their way through the
village from one lodge to another, that no one might be
slighted.

Some limit might doubtless be found at all times for the
food-taking powers of the civilized man, but for these savage
people no limit seemed possible. The honored guests of
the occasion had fasted for days, and now they feasted in
every lodge of the village, to compensate for the loss. Not
formal feasting of small amounts here and there, but great
earnest feasting, such as hunger induces.

When the darkness came on, an old warrior took his seat
on the ground, near the center of the village, and began to
beat on a drum as a signal for the dancing to begin.

The people at once flocked around him, and made a great
fire with the fuel which the squaws and the peons had
gathered.

After some time had elapsed a single warrior came forward and took his place near the drummer. He stood still
for some time and then threw off his blanket and began to
move back and forth, keeping time in his motions with the

dull, heavy blows of the drum. He slowly became more absorbed in his purpose and at length beat on the ground with his feet and swayed his nearly nude body to and fro, with increasing animation. Then he began a low chant, which slowly increased in volume and time until the supreme moment had come, when he suddenly broke out in the stiff, jerky motions of the Indian dance.

Several young warriors sprang forward at once, when this consummation was reached, to join their companion. They took their places in order one after the other, in a long single line, and began to dance and to chant in accord with their leader.

At a signal from the drummer the dancers changed places or moved forward or backward in column or line. Sometimes they danced forward in a long single line, and then followed each other to the left or right.

Then they moved to the rear and turned all together and danced forward once more. They circled and wheeled and advanced and retreated and moved in column and line, with quick measured motions and solemn demeanor, until at last the drum ceased and ended the dance for a time.

A few squaws hastened forward when the dance was concluded, and swept the dust from the ground with green cedar bushes and brooms made of reeds.

When they had completed their work, the drum sounded again, and a single warrior sprang forward and began the dance as before.

Then other dances succeeded, following each other with brief intermission and unvarying sameness until late in the night.

The runner To-mé, almost worn out by fatigue and barely awake, sat in his place and watched the dances. The night had well worn away when Che-no, the dwarf,

pushed his way through the crowd and came softly behind
him and pulled at his blanket. The runner turned quickly
about to see who in the throng had disturbed him. His
gaze fell at once on the troubled face of the dwarf.

"Che-no would speak with the warrior," he said quietly,
"but he cannot speak here."

"Let the dwarf go away," said the runner, waving him
back with his hand. "Why should he speak to To-mé?"

"The young squaws and the peons have grown very
bold," said an old warrior who sat by the side of To-mé.

But Che-no would not go away. He pulled again at the
blanket, and plead piteously for permission to speak to
To-mé. At last the runner got up from his seat, and
went away from the people, closely followed by the dwarf.
When they had gone out of sight, the runner stopped suddenly, and turning about, exclaimed harshly,

"Let the peon speak quickly."

"Nah-nee-ta has been sold," said the dwarf. "When
the light comes again she will go to the lodge of the chief."

"And who bade the peon speak those words to To-mé?"
he asked, sternly.

"Che-no speaks to the warrior because the girl cries in
the lodge," he said, sadly, "and the heart of the peon is
heavy."

To-mé was much troubled at the words of the peon, and
walked back and forth with evident emotion. He had
feared from the first, when Me-su-la had informed him of
the visit of the woman, that she would succeed in her purpose, and eventually accomplish what now had occurred.

"The medicine man spake," said the peon, "and Po-lone
was ill-pleased with his words."

"What words did he speak?" asked the runner.

"Che-no knows not, but the woman was troubled, and
held down her head as she rode on the trail."

"Me-ra!" cried the runner, between his closed teeth. "They obey not the customs of the nation. They close their ears to the words they should hear. They would steal the girl now from To-mé, if they could."

"Hist!" cried the peon, in a whisper. "Che-no hears footsteps."

"Yea," said the runner, absorbed in his thoughts. "Some one of the people come near. Let Che-no now hasten to return to the fire and sit down near the woman. When she comes to her lodge, Che-no must come on before."

The dwarf hastened away and quickly disappeared in the darkness. As soon as he was gone, the runner proceeded to the lodge of the woman.

Nah-nee-ta had conformed to the custom of her people, and retired to the lodge of her mother, where she waited, as the custom required, for the coming of her master. She had fallen asleep on her robe when To-mé arrived at the lodge, but his voice quickly awakened her, and she sat up on the robe and gazed at the runner in utter amazement.

"Why does Nah-nee-ta sleep now in her lodge," he asked softly, "when all the people watch the dancers at the fire?"

"Nah-nee-ta has been sold," she said sadly, "and waits for her master."

"Then the words of Me-su-la, that Nah-nee-ta should come to the lodge of To-mé, were not good," he said bitterly.

"Nah-nee-ta knows not," she replied.

"She will be happy in the lodge of the chief," said the runner.

The girl made no reply, but bowed down her head, and covered her face with her hands.

"Me-ra!" cried the runner, "Let Nah-nee-ta make ready and ride with To-mé to the land of the Utes."

"Nay," said the girl, "Po-lone would be angry."

"To-mé's horses are swift," urged the runner, "and Nah-nee-ta would soon be far away from the woman."

She made no reply, and To-mé continued.

"Let Nah-nee-ta speak quick. The dancers are weary and Po-lone will soon come to her lodge."

"Nah-nee-ta will go," said the girl, "Let To-mé make haste with the horses."

He sprang out of the lodge scarcely waiting to hear all her words, and ran to the corral for the horses. Unfastening them quickly, he led them away as rapidly as possible. But the animal he had ridden through the village with the chief that day, could scarcely move forward at all. It gave him, however, but little concern, for the horse had doubtless grown lame from hardover work, and a few rapid steps would drive the lameness away. He sprang on its back and forced it along, leading the other horse after.

When he arrived at the lodge, Nah-nee-ta was ready and anxiously awaiting his return. Dismounting at once, he raised her up quickly on the back of the horse which he led, and then mounted again on the other. A moment thereafter they rode slowly away to the north.

They had scarcely accomplished their escape from the village, when a warrior ran up to the lodge, and glanced hastily within. Then darting back he looked hurriedly around, and catching an indistinct view of the horses, as they went out of sight in the darkness, he called quickly.

"Who rides?"

No answer came back except the quick patter of feet, as the horses sprang forward on the trail. Comprehending at once what had happened, the warrior gazed for a moment in the direction in which the horses had gone, and then aroused all the village by his yells. Several warriors came running to the lodge, with the chief at their head, to learn the cause of the alarm.

"Why does Mal-tush-malo frighten the people with his yells?" asked the chief.

"To-mé, the runner, has ridden to the north with the daughter of Po-lone," he replied, "and Mal-tush-malo cried out that the people might know."

No one in the village was more surprised than the chief. He had expected some desperate interference, and had set the old warrior Mal-tush-malo to watch, that it might be promptly met and defeated. But such a bold act as this, in violation of all tribal customs, had not been deemed possible. The chief grew enraged as he thought of the injury thus done to himself, and the bad name it would bring on his clan, and turning at last to his warriors, he shouted,

"Make ready to ride. The customs of the nation have been broken without any cause, and the maiden which the chief had just bought, has been stolen from the midst of the clan. Are the warriors of Mariano all squaws, whom no one now fears, that such a thing can be done? Make haste," he cried violently, "make haste with full quivers, that this evil deed may be wiped out with blood."

The warriors hurried away to their lodges as soon as the chief ceased to speak, and sent their squaws in hot haste for the horses. As quickly as the animals could be brought from the corral, and made ready to ride, the eager warriors sprang on their backs and rode rapidly away to join their companions.

"Me-ra !" cried the chief. "Let few arrows fly, lest the girl may be harmed. Straight arrows fly crooked sometimes in the dark."

Then turning his horse to the north, he rode rapidly away, followed closely by his warriors.

Only two routes existed over which horsemen could travel, in journeying from the village to the north. One led through the cañon and the other through the pasture grounds of Me-su-la. The chief galloped rapidly forward until he reached the broad trail that branched off to the left, and ran up through the cañon. Stopping here for a moment to examine the path, he discovered that the runner had passed on to the north, by the trail that led through the pasture grounds of Me-su-la.

The chief was well pleased that the runner had chosen this route. It would be almost impossible for him now to escape from the mountain-bound valley through which the trail ran, and the pursuit could be pushed even more rapidly than before. But it was yet barely possible that he might turn to the left, on the top of the mesa, and go down by the trail to the cañon beyond, and so find his way to the great open valley, where pursuit would be tedious until daylight had come. To prevent the success of such an attempt, the chief dispatched a few warriors to ride quickly through the cañon, and then ascend by the trail to the mesa. As soon as they were gone, he continued the pursuit, and galloped on rapidly to the north.

In the meantime To-mé and Nah-nee-ta, fully aware of their danger, hastened forward as rapidly as possible. They comprehended at once, when their flight was discovered, that quick pursuit would be made, and that their escape all depended on the speed of their horses. They had gone on for sometime, and had accomplished a long distance, when to their utter dismay, the lame horse stumbled forward, and then stopped altogether and lay down on the ground. To-mé, in despair, beat the horse with his bow and urged him to rise, but all to no purpose. The poor creature was completely exhausted, and refused to get up on its feet. After much valuable time had been lost in this way, To-mé suddenly came close to the girl, where she sat on her horse, and said eagerly,

"Nah-nee-ta is wise. Let her hearken to the words of To-mé. One horse is not enough to escape from the warriors. Nah-nee-ta must return to the lodge of the woman, and To-mé will hasten on foot to escape in the mountain."

"Nay, nay," said the girl with great earnestness. "Nah-nee-ta will go with To-mé. She will run after on foot, and hide in the mountain, but never go back to Po-lone."

To-mé stood undecided for a moment, and then sprang up behind her, and urged the horse forward once more.

Their progress was now less rapid than before, and To-mé often sprang down on the ground, and ran forward on foot, to save the strength of the horse for a great final effort, if such should be needed. They came at last to the mesa, and rode hastily across it to the dark forest beyond. As they approached near the forest, the quick ear of the runner caught the dull heavy tramping of horses feet on the trail, some distance behind them.

"The warriors ride hard," he said calmly. "They are not far away." He paused for a moment, and then continued with firmness. "Nah-nee-ta can go no further. To-mé has done wrong. He has stolen Nah-nee-ta from the lodge of her mother, and she must return while she can."

"Nay, Nay," she replied, sobbing piteously while she spoke. "Nah-nee-ta will never go back. She will follow To-mé while she lives."

"Nah-nee-ta shall never go back," he replied, giving way to her earnest appeal. "Turn the horse to the left," he added quickly, "and keep close in the shadow of the forest."

They galloped forward with greater speed than before,
and the sound of the tramping was soon lost in the distance. For a brief period they indulged in the hope that
their pursuers had gone on to the north, and that much valuable time would be gained before their trail could be found.
But this cheering hope had scarcely been awakened, when
the dull, heavy tramping once more could be heard, some
distance behind them. It gradually came nearer, and grew
more distinct, until at last it seemed almost upon them.
But To-mé still boldly pushed forward hoping yet to be able
to get down in the cañon, and escape to the valley.

He had scarcely gone past the great rocks where the
chiefs came at times to make medicine together, when several mounted warriors came suddenly in view, a short distance before him. With loud yells of triumph, and arrows
poised on their bows, they rushed instantly forward towards
him. The loud yells of the warriors, and the rushing of
the horses, appalled the stout heart of Nah-nee-ta, and
rudely crushed out her last hope of escape. She dropped
the reins from her hands and fell helpless in the arms of
To-mé. The horse reared on its haunches, and, turning
quickly about, fled in terror before its pursuers. To-mé
seized the reins and attempted in vain to direct the course
of its flight. It ran forward blindly, bewildered by fear
and at last dashed through the opening between the great
rocks, and fell headlong in the place that had sunk beneath
the horse of the Apaches. It struggled at once to its feet
and springing out of the hole, galloped madly away through
the bushes.

To-mé clung to his seat until the horse had fallen down,
and then sprang from its back with the girl in his arms.
Apprehending some danger from the struggles of the animal
in its attempts to get up, he hastily drew back and crouched

down on the ground. As his pursuers came nearer he drew further back, to hide in the dense darkness behind him.

Nah-nee-ta recovered slowly from the deadly stupor into which she had fallen, and some time had elapsed before she was fully restored. Then recalling at once the cause of her terror, she sprang on her knees, and attempted to look about her.

"Where are they, To-mé?" she cried, loudly. "The warriors ! Where are they?"

"Hist !" he answered hurriedly. "They are not far away, and Nah-nee-ta speaks loud."

"It is dark," she whispered nervously, "and the stars have gone out. Where has To-mé hid now from the light?"

"To-mé knows not," he replied. "The horse ran between the great rocks, and fell down in a hole, and To-mé crawled quickly in the darkness, to hide from the warriors."

"Me-ra !" cried the girl, and seizing the hand of the runner, she held it towards a small opening, through which a faint light could be seen. "Me-ra !" she cried with great earnestness. "To-mé has crawled into the cavern, beneath the great mesa."

He raised quickly to his feet, and held up his hand until it touched the cold stone overhead.

"Yea," he said quietly, as he sat down by her side. "To-mé has crawled into the cavern. The Great Spirit is good."

"Nay, nay," she replied, much excited. "An evil thing lives in the cavern. Let To-mé make haste to escape."

"Me-ra," he said softly. "To-mé wears a charm that the medicine man gave him. Evil things that come near it, are turned into stone. The warriors search now in the bushes, and on the mountain, and To-mé must stay where he is, until they have all gone away."

Assured by these confident words of the runner, Nah-nee-ta sat down, and rested her head on his shoulder. With

most wonderful condescension on the part of a warrior, he
permitted this act of affection, and softly stroked her dark
hair with his hand.   They sat thus together, awaiting with
patience what the future might bring, supremely indifferent,
apparently, to what it might be.

At last the day dawned, and the light slowly entered the
mouth of the cavern.   To-mé arose to his feet when he
caught the first glimpse of the objects about him, and feeling before him on the ground with his bow, moved slowly
back in the cavern.

"Where does To-mé go now?" asked the girl, as she
moved on at his side.

"To find some other opening, if possible," he replied,
"that goes out of the cavern."

They moved on for some time, groping their way through
the darkness, until they grew weary and almost discouraged
from further attempt.   But at length they caught sight of
a faint glimmer of light in the distance before them, and at
once hastened forward towards it, overjoyed to escape from
the death-like embrace of the darkness.   Gazing upward at
the rocky roof overhead, they observed a narrow fissure
through which the light streamed.

To-mé stopped in surprise when he emerged from the
darkness, scarcely able to believe that the narrow passage
before him could possibly be the great cavern of the
stories and the legends of his people.   It was scarcely wider
than twice the length of his bow, and the roof was almost
within reach of his hand.   He looked with curious care on
the walls, and traced with his finger deep lines that seemed
worn by swift running water.   He went on a short distance
further, and then stopped abruptly before a narrow fissure,
filled with a dull, greyish substance from which portions
had been broken and carried away.   As he traced the nar-

row fissure from the roof to the floor, his eyes fell at last upon a sharp iron bar with a hole in the center, through which a long wooden handle had been thrust. He had seen such a thing once before in the hands of some Mexican traders, who had come to exchange their wares with his people. Comprehending its purpose, he seized it at once, and struck the sharp point in the substance, and broke out a piece from the mass.

"What has To-mé found now?" asked the girl, much surprised.

"The evil thing," he said quickly, "that lives in the cavern."

"It has turned into stone when the charm has come near it," she said anxiously.

"Yea," he replied. "It has turned into stone. To-mé knows now," he earnestly continued. "To-mé knows now, why the chiefs come so often to make medicine in the rocks, and why their herds are so large, and their great silver buttons so plenty. It is silver, Nah-nee-ta."

He threw down the pick with a great show of anger, and moved on again in the darkness, with the girl close behind him. They had gone on for some time, when again a faint glimmer of light could be seen. It increased as they advanced, until at last the whole cavern opened out to the light.

As they came near to the opening, To-mé motioned to the girl with his hand, to stop where she stood, and falling down on his face, he crawled cautiously forward. At first his gaze fell on the ragged face of a mountain some distance beyond, but as he drew nearer it swept slowly down and rested at last in the cañon Bo-neet. Many people from the village had gathered in the cañon, and the murmur of their voices reached the ear of the runner. Several warriors had

crowded upon the rocks, at the base of the mountain, and
stood with poised arrows, watching intently at the mouth
of the cavern.   He lay for some time curiously watching the
scene, and coolly counting the warriors who stood ready to
shoot.

At last the girl grew impatient at the delay of the runner,
and stepped noiselessly forward and stood in full view in the
opening and gazed down in the cañon.   Wild yells of
triumph rang at once through the air, and many cruel
arrows whizzed mercilessly into the opening.   With a loud
scream of terror, Nah-nee-ta loosed her hold on the wall, and
turned quickly about to escape in the cavern.   As she turned
on the smooth water-worn rocks, her foothold gave way
and she fell on her face.   To-mé sprang to his feet and
seized hold of her blanket, but it gave way in his hands,
and she went instantly over, and fell through the air to the
bottom of the cavern.

Horror-stricken and bewildered, To-mé stood for a moment
like one in a dream, before he was able to comprehend fully
the terrible event that had happened.   Then, almost crazed
by his grief, he resolved quickly to spring after the girl, and
meet his fate at her side.   He paused for an instant,
diverted from his purpose by the loud cries of the people,
and falling once more on the floor of the cavern, he crawled
to the edge, and looked down in the cañon.   The squaws
were already bearing the body away, and the warriors still
stood in their places, with arrows poised ready to shoot.

A change slowly came over the face of the runner as he lay
watching the warriors who sought for his life.

"They are dogs," he murmured bitterly.   "They have
killed the poor maiden, and wait now with their arrows to
shoot at To-mé."

Rising quickly to his feet, he uttered a wild yell, and disappeared in the cavern.   The warriors answered his yell

with their arrows, and comprehending his desperate purpose they hastened at once by the nearest trail up the great wall to the top of the mesa.

All the warriors except one, and all the people of the village, who had come out in the morning, had been sent by the chief to the cañon. He alone with old Mal-tush-malo, guarded the opening to the cavern between the great rocks.

When the warriors reached the mesa, they ran with great speed to the mountain, and dashed through the bushes with breathless haste to the opening. But the last struggle was over before they arrived, and To-mé sorely wounded, had escaped to the mountain. Old Mal-tush-malo lay dead on the ground with an arrow in his heart, and the chief, pale and bleeding from the wounds of a knife, lay helpless by his side.

Several warriors at once started in pursuit of To-mé, and followed his trail across the great mountain to the pasture grounds of Me-su-la, and then far away to the east, where they lost it at last in a wild, rocky cañon.

As soon as the pursuers were gone out of sight, the chief bade his warriors bring stones to the opening, and fill it up to the top, that no one might enter the evil place any more.

XVII

The years slowly succeeded each other after these tragic events had occurred, and no tidings ever came from To-mé.

A vague rumor, it is true, found ready credence with the people after several years had elapsed, that he had made his home with the Comanches, and had become a great chief.

Many changes in the meantime had taken place in the nation.

The clan of Mariano had grown great and rich, and made lasting peace with its neighbors.

Mexican traders at times pitched their camps near the border, and traded in safety with the people.

At last one bolder than the others, ventured across the vague line, and journeyed slowly along on the bank of the Puerco. He was permitted to advance until he came near the village, when a runner from the chief bade him stop where he was.

The anxious people soon flocked in a great crowd about him to examine the wonderful things he had brought to exchange for their blankets and silver. They feasted their eyes on the bright-colored beads and the curious tools made of iron and the shining trinkets of brass, which he quickly displayed to their view.

He was accompanied by a Ute, who had lived for sometime with one of the great clans in the north, and who had joined him a few days before. The Ute had fought lately in a desperate battle somewhere, and had received a great wound from a knife on the side of his face. A broad bandage of buckskin, yet bloody from the wound, was bound on his head, and partially concealed his features from view.

At times he made answer to the questions that were asked him, but his speech was much labored and his words indistinct by reason of his wound.

Among the last from the village came the woman Po-lone, and joining with the crowd, she stood looking at the tempting wares of the trader. Her eyes fell at last on the Ute, and she quickly asked who he was.

"Some vagabond Ute," said a voice, "who has followed the trader to the village."

She watched him attentively for awhile, and then turned away with a sigh. There was something in the manner of the poor ragged creature that awakened sad memories of the past. But who he might be, or why his presence recalled these sad things, she could not even conjecture. Unable to control her sad thoughts, she returned soon again to the place where he stood. She heard him speak as she approached, and at the sound of his voice the troubled expression passed at once from her face. Hurrying quickly to his side, she waited impatiently until no one observed her, and then whispered softly,

"Po-lone hears the voice of To-mé."

"What means the strange words of the squaw?" he asked hoarsely.

"To-mé knows," she replied. "Po-lone has grown very weary with her long years of waiting," she continued, "but her heart is glad now, because To-mé has come."

"In the nation of the Comanches," he said slowly, "a warrior called To-mé has become a great chief. Does the woman speak now of the chief of the Comanches?"

"To-mé knows," she replied, and then asked very softly. "Does the chief ever wish for Po-lone in his lodge?"

"Yea," he answered quickly, "To-mé's heart will be glad when Po-lone comes to his lodge."

The village moved often from one place to another in search of new pastures for the herds, and now delayed only until the trader was gone to move on again.

As the day wore away Po-lone rode from her lodge to visit the grounds which the chief had selected for the new village site. She was followed by Che-no, the dwarf, carrying blankets and robes and some food from the lodge, to provide for the night if a delay should occur.

When the sun had gone down, the trader packed up his wares, and the people returned slowly to their homes in the village. As soon as they were gone, the vagabond Ute set out for the north, to return to his people. When he was well out of sight, he tore the bandage from his face, and changing his course followed after the woman.

He found her at last, and the two rode away followed by the dwarf, and were never heard of again in the nation. But the story still lives in the lodges of the clans, how To-mé, the runner, came back in disguise and stole the woman from the village while the chief Mariano exchanged his robes with the trader.